Fisher Investments on Health Care

FISHER INVESTMENTS PRESS

Fisher Investments Press brings the research, analysis, and market intelligence of Fisher Investments' research team, headed by CEO and *New York Times* best-selling author Ken Fisher, to all investors. The Press covers a range of investing and market-related topics for a wide audience—from novices to enthusiasts to professionals.

Books by Ken Fisher
Debunkery
How to Smell a Rat
The Ten Roads to Riches
The Only Three Questions That Count
100 Minds That Made the Market
The Wall Street Waltz
Super Stocks

Fisher Investments Series
Own the World by
Aaron Anderson

20/20 Money by
Michael Hanson

Fisher Investments On Series
Fisher Investments on Energy
Fisher Investments on Materials
Fisher Investments on Consumer Staples
Fisher Investments on Industrials
Fisher Investments on Emerging Markets
Fisher Investments on Technology
Fisher Investments on Consumer Discretionary
Fisher Investments on Utilities
Fisher Investments on Health Care

FISHER
INVESTMENTS
PRESS

Fisher Investments on Health Care

Fisher Investments Press

with

Michael Kelly and
Andrew S. Teufel

John Wiley & Sons, Inc.

Published by John Wiley & Sons, Inc., Hoboken, New Jersey.
Published simultaneously in Canada.

Important Disclaimers: This book reflects personal opinions, viewpoints and analyses of the authors and should not be regarded as a description of advisory services provided by Fisher Investments or performance returns of any Fisher Investments client. Fisher Investments manages its clients' accounts using a variety of investment techniques and strategies not necessarily discussed in this book. Nothing in this book constitutes investment advice or any recommendation with respect to a particular country, sector, industry, security or portfolio of securities. All information is impersonal and not tailored to the circumstances or investment needs of any specific person.

Limit of Liability/Disclaimer of Warranty: While the publisher and authors have used their best efforts in preparing this book, they make no representations or warranties with respect to the accuracy or completeness of the contents of this book and specifically disclaim any implied warranties of merchantability or fitness for a particular purpose. No warranty may be created or extended by sales representatives or written sales materials. The advice and strategies contained herein may not be suitable for your situation. You should consult with a professional where appropriate. Neither the publisher nor author shall be liable for any loss of profit or any other commercial damages, including but not limited to special, incidental, consequential, or other damages.

For general information on our other products and services or for technical support, please contact our Customer Care Department within the United States at (800) 762-2974, outside the United States at (317) 572-3993 or fax (317) 572-4002.

Wiley also publishes its books in a variety of electronic formats. Some content that appears in print may not be available in electronic books. For more information about Wiley products, visit our web site at www.wiley.com.

Library of Congress Cataloging-in-Publication Data:

    Fisher investments on health care / Fisher Investments Press ; with Michael Kelly and Andrew S. Teufel.
       p. cm.—(Fisher investments on)
    Includes bibliographical references and index.
    ISBN 978-0-470-52705-4 (cloth); ISBN 978-1-118-00981-9 (ebk);
    ISBN 978-1-118-00982-6 (ebk); ISBN 978-1-118-00983-3 (ebk)
      1. Medical economics.   I. Kelly, Michael.   II. Teufel, Andrew S.
    III. Fisher Investments.
    RA410.F575 2011
    338.4'33621—dc22   2010042181

Printed in the United States of America

10 9 8 7 6 5 4 3 2 1

Contents

Foreword

*F*isher Investments on Health Care is the eighth in a series of investing guides from Fisher Investments Press—the first-ever imprint from
a money manager. While reading the entire series would be a worthwhile endeavor for serious students of capital markets—covering the
full breadth of capital market analysis—each book can stand on its own
in its area. This book (and the series) presents a usable, top-down strategy for analyzing standard investing sectors (Energy, Materials, Consumer Staples, Industrials, etc.) as well as other investing regions and
categories. This book is on Health Care—currently about 8 percent of
total world stocks (as measured by the MSCI All Country index).

When folks hear "Health Care," they probably think pharmaceuticals and insurers. And that's right—but the sector also covers equipment makers, hospitals, biotechnology, distributors, services, supplies,
technology, and life sciences. It may seem stodgy, but there's massive,
non-stop, life-saving innovation going on in drugs and equipment,
and also many Health Care sub-industries.

Thanks to major US legislation passed in 2010, Health Care is
certain to be a hot and often controversial topic for many years to come.
That legislation (and any later legislation to change, repeal, clarify, or
what-have-you 2010's legislation) will impact Health Care firms in
ways legislators couldn't have possibly imagined—and certainly aren't
fully fathomable at this time. But the job of a Health Care analyst
isn't to decide whether legislation is good or bad, or to debate how the
sector *should* be regulated. Instead, it is to always rationally assess the
existing landscape, whether it's likely to change, and how that likely
impacts demand (and alternatively supply) for Health Care stocks.

Plus, Health Care is no stranger to legislation! Think of all the regulation aimed at pharmaceutical firms, insurers, medical device makers, hospitals, and so on. And Health Care firms are frequently targets for lawsuits. Nothing new about that! Understanding how regulatory and legal matters impact the sector and its industries is vital to making better forecasts. This book shows you how and provides a fundamental framework.

Don't let regulation scare you off. Health Care plays a vital portfolio role—it's a classically defensive sector. When times are tough, folks still take aspirin and need hips replaced. But when times are flush, you generally don't double up on insulin or heart medication. Hence, investors see Health Care as a refuge—it tends to do better than the market during bear markets while lagging in the sizzling times. In an overly simple sense, Health Care can be thought of in just that way—a great thing to own when other forms of defensive stocks beat the market, but not so great when defensive stocks lag in general. But Health Care has certainly had periods when it outperformed during a bull market—as it did in the late 1990s! It is fairly defensive, but innovation can be a tremendous driver too. This book explains the disparate drivers for Health Care's many industries, and how to know if the sector as a whole (and underlying industries) is likely to out- or underperform—no matter the market conditions.

And it's wrong to think Health Care is inherently less risky just because it's overall more defensive than sectors like Consumer Discretionary, Energy, or Materials. Or that Health Care should get better or worse returns over the long term. Over the long term, finance theory says all equity categories should net pretty similar returns when properly accounted for—though traveling drastically different paths over the short to intermediate term. Ultimately, given enough time, newly created supply or the destruction of existing supply tends to equalize categories. In the nearer term, demand tends to drive stock prices, but longer term (what may seem for most like an eternity but really isn't), supply swamps demand for that category. (For a more detailed discussion on the general process of how supply is almost all powerful in affecting stock prices in the very long term, see my 2007 John Wiley book *The Only Three Questions That Count*, pages 240–250.) That's why a good portfolio is broadly diversified, and why this book (and the entire series) can help you learn to be a better investor.

Don't expect to find any "get rich quick" ideas or hot stock tips in this book. Such a thing doesn't exist—someone telling you otherwise is selling you something unhealthy. Rather, this book provides a workable, repeatable framework for increasing the likelihood of finding profitable opportunities in the Health Care sector. And the good news is the investing methodology presented here works for all investing sectors and the broader market. This methodology should serve you not only this year or next, but the whole of your investing career. So good luck and enjoy the journey.

KEN FISHER
CEO of Fisher Investments
Forbes Portfolio Strategy Columnist
Author of the *New York Times*
Best Sellers,
How to Smell a Rat, The Ten Roads to Riches, and
The Only Three Questions That Count

Preface

The *Fisher Investments On* series is designed to provide individual investors, students, and aspiring investment professionals the tools necessary to understand and analyze investment opportunities, primarily for investing in global stocks.

Within the framework of a "top-down" investment method (more on that in Chapter 7), each guide is an easily accessible primer to economic sectors, regions, or other components of the global stock market. While this guide is specifically on Health Care, the basic investment methodology is applicable for analyzing any global sector, regardless of the current macroeconomic environment.

Why a top-down method? Vast evidence shows high-level, or "macro," investment decisions are ultimately more important portfolio performance drivers than individual stocks. In other words, before picking stocks, investors can benefit greatly by first deciding whether stocks are the best investment relative to other assets (like bonds or cash), and then choosing categories of stocks most likely to perform best on a forward-looking basis.

For example, a Tech sector stock picker in the mid to late 1990s probably saw his picks soar. But in 2000 to 2003, his picks were likely decimated. Was he just smarter in 1998 and 1999? Did his analysis turn bad somehow? Unlikely. What mattered most was stocks in general, and especially Tech stocks, did relatively great in the 1990s, but Tech crashed in 2000, and US stocks overall did lousy in the 2001 to 2002 bear market. In other words, a top-down perspective on the broader economy was key to navigating markets—stock picking just wasn't as important.

Fisher Investments on Health Care will guide you in making top-down investment decisions specifically for the Health Care sector. It shows how to determine better times to invest in Health Care, what Health Care industries are likelier to do best, and how individual stocks can benefit in various environments. The global Health Care sector is complex, covering many industries and countries with unique characteristics. Using our framework, you will be better-equipped to identify their differences, spot opportunities, and avoid major pitfalls.

This book takes a global approach to Health Care investing. Most US investors typically invest the majority of their assets in domestic securities; they forget America is less than half of the world stock market by weight—over 50 percent of investment opportunities are outside our borders. While a larger proportion of the world's Health Care weight is based in the US, many companies derive a significant portion of profits overseas. Given the vast market landscape and diverse geographic operations, it's vital to have a global perspective when investing in Health Care today.

USING YOUR HEALTH CARE GUIDE

This guide is designed in three parts. Part I, Getting Started in Health Care, discusses vital sector basics including the history of major developments in Health Care. We'll also discuss sector-level drivers that ultimately influence stock prices.

Part II, Next Steps: Health Care Details, walks through the next step of sector analysis. We'll take you through the global Health Care sector investment universe and its diverse components. The Health Care sector itself presents 3 industry groups, 8 industries, and 16 sub-industries. Various firms are driven by enterprise spending, others by consumers, and some by infrastructure build-outs. Many are leveraged to combinations of these, yet others are leveraged to none. We will take you through the eight industries in detail, how they operate, and what drives profitability—to give you the tools to determine which industry will most likely outperform or underperform looking forward.

Part II also details many of the challenges Health Care firms face, including historical examples of how these challenges have been met and overcome. Moreover, we'll discuss certain products and manufacturing processes used today, as well as how they're advancing through new and emerging technologies.

Part III, Thinking Like a Portfolio Manager, delves into a top-down investment methodology and individual security analysis. You'll learn to ask important questions like: What are the most important elements to consider when analyzing semiconductor and PC firms? What are the greatest risks and red flags? This book gives you a five-step process to help differentiate firms so you can identify ones with a greater probability of outperforming. We'll also discuss a few investment strategies to help determine when and how to overweight specific industries within the sector.

Fisher Investments on Health Care won't give you a "silver bullet" for picking the right Health Care stocks. The fact is the "right" Health Care stocks will be different in different times and situations. Instead, this guide provides a framework for understanding the sector and its industries so that you can be dynamic and find information the market hasn't yet priced in. There won't be any stock recommendations, target prices, political stances, or even a suggestion whether now is a good time to be invested in the Health Care sector. The goal is to provide you with tools to make these decisions for yourself, now and in the future. Ultimately, our aim is to give you the framework for repeated, successful investing. Enjoy.

Acknowledgments

A number of colleagues and friends deserve tremendous praise and thanks for helping make this book a reality. We would like to extend our tremendous thanks to Ken Fisher for providing the opportunity to write this book. Jeff Silk deserves our thanks for constantly challenging us to improve and presenting new and insightful questions as fast as we can answer them. Our colleagues at Fisher Investments also deserve tremendous thanks for continually sharing their wealth of knowledge, insights, and analysis. Without these people the very concept of this book would never have been possible.

We owe a huge debt of gratitude to Lara Hoffmans and Michael Hanson, without whose guidance, patience, and editing contributions this book would not have been completed. We'd like to thank Evelyn Chea for her hard work and thoroughness in editing and assistance with citations, sources, and copyediting. Without Leila Amiri we would have been utterly lost in our attempts to implement graphics and images. A special thanks to Brian Kepp, Roger Bohl, Charles Thies, and Brad Pyles for their contributions to data and content. Marc Haberman, Molly Lienesch, and Fabrizio Ornani were also instrumental in the creation of Fisher Investments Press, which created the infrastructure behind this book. And hearty thanks to Fred Harring, Tom Fishel, and Nicole Gerrard for giving generously of their time to review the book. Of course this book would also not be possible without our data vendors, so we owe a big thank you to Reuters and Global Financial Data. We'd also like to thank our team at John Wiley & Sons, for their support and guidance throughout this project, especially Laura Walsh and Kelly O'Connor.

Michael Kelly would also like to specifically thank his wife Megan and parents Michael and Patti for their constant love and support.

I

GETTING STARTED IN HEALTH CARE

1

HEALTH CARE BASICS

Shane is having dinner with his wife Emily when he notices a strange numbness in his arm keeps him from picking up his fork. He tries to tell Emily, but numbness in his face slurs his speech. Worried, she immediately calls 911, and an ambulance arrives and rushes him to the nearest hospital. Doctors run various tests and determine plaque formation in his carotid artery is preventing adequate blood flow to his brain, causing a stroke. To treat Shane, doctors will perform a procedure called carotid angioplasty and stenting, where a small balloon will open the clogged carotid artery, and a stent (a thin, metal mesh tube) will be inserted to keep the artery open. Shane is moved and placed on a stainless steel table in a sanitized operating room. Doctors wash their hands, put on their scrubs and gloves, and use various tools and equipment to perform the procedure. Shane successfully recovers and heads to the local pharmacy to pick up his newly prescribed medicine. He later receives the bill and works with his insurance company to pay for the services rendered. Shane is thankful Emily recognized the early signs of a stroke.

This is more than a simple anecdote with a happy ending—it's an illustration of how Health Care products and services impact our

Table 1.1   Health Care Sector Impact

Interaction With	Health Care Sector Involvement
Ambulance	Performed by a Health Care Services company
Hospital	Run by a Health Care Facilities company
Diagnostic machines used to run tests	Made by Life Sciences and Health Care Equipment firms
Lab test	Performed by a Health Care Services company
Balloon and stent	Manufactured by a Health Care Equipment company
Stainless steel table, knives, and gloves	Manufactured by Health Care Equipment and Supplies companies and delivered to hospitals through Health Care Distributors
Prescription drugs	Manufactured by a Pharmaceuticals firm
Health insurance company	Run by a Managed Care provider

lives. Every event, interaction, and item in Shane's situation used products and services from the Health Care sector. Table 1.1 lists just some of the Health Care products and services he encountered.

This book covers investment opportunities in the Health Care sector, as well as how to better incorporate a Health Care allocation into a broader portfolio. Many of the firms making people's lives healthier are publicly traded and can be an integral part of your portfolio. Of the 10 standard investing sectors, Health Care arguably plays the most critical role—literally—in daily life. Moreover, in recent years, health care—its availability, cost, and how it should be delivered—are among the most hotly debated topics around the world. After all, it was Mahatma Gandhi who said, "It is health that is the real wealth and not pieces of gold and silver."

This doesn't suggest Health Care is inherently superior to other sectors (Energy, Materials, Industrials, Consumer Staples, etc.)—it isn't. But Health Care, like each sector, has unique attributes leading both to outperformance and underperformance depending upon economic, market, and industry-specific conditions. There will be periods when Health Care performs very well relative to the broader market and periods when it lags.

While health care can be a politically touchy subject and can foster great ethical debate, the aim of the book isn't to support one ideology or another. Rather, the goal is to help you gain a basic understanding of the Health Care sector—its components, drivers, and challenges—and serve as a general guide for better Health Care investing. Wherever possible, we'll also help you think critically about the sector to generate your own views rather than just dictating rules. Successfully investing in Health Care firms doesn't require an advanced degree in medicine. Instead, you need a firm grasp of the laws of supply and demand and an understanding of what drives the earnings and stock prices of Health Care firms.

HEALTH CARE BASICS

Figure 1.1 shows how the sector composition of the MSCI All Country World Index (ACWI) is broken down. The ACWI index covers the entire globe, including emerging markets, and is currently the broadest representation of global stocks. The index is capitalization weighted, meaning larger firms have more weight. Health Care currently accounts for 9 percent of the index and is one of the

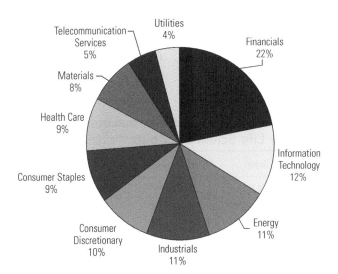

Figure 1.1   Breakdown of the MSCI All Country World Index
Source: Thomson Reuters, MSCI Inc.,[1] as of 12/31/2009.

smaller sectors by weight. That doesn't make it unimportant, however. Further, sector weights may differ among various indexes, as you will see in subsequent chapters. And as sectors go in and out of favor, their relative weights can change, sometimes tremendously.

What does the Health Care sector look like from a high level? Not all health-related firms belong in the sector. For example, food, some consumer products, and retail pharmacies belong in the Consumer Staples sector, while some Industrial sector conglomerates, such as General Electric and Siemens, own large Health Care equipment and diagnostic divisions. This isn't a hard and fast rule, but classification as a Health Care firm largely depends upon how much health-related revenues and profits comprise a firm's overall sales and earnings.

Because Health Care has many diverse industries, it's split into two broad groups (as defined by the Global Industry Classification Standard [GICS] classification system):

- Pharmaceuticals, Biotechnology & Life Sciences
- Health Care Equipment & Services

Pharmaceuticals, Biotechnology & Life Sciences, the larger group, includes firms involved in the discovery, development, manufacturing, and distribution of prescription drugs. It also includes firms supporting the drug discovery process, as well as those that serve firms outside the health care business by testing the quality of

Table 1.2 Largest Firms in the Pharmaceuticals, Biotechnology & Life Sciences Group

Name	Ticker	Market Cap ($Mil)	Country	Industry
Johnson & Johnson	JNJ	$177,714	US	Pharmaceuticals
Pfizer	PFE	$146,785	US	Pharmaceuticals
Novartis	NVS	$144,165	Switzerland	Pharmaceuticals
Roche Holding	RHHBY	$119,482	Switzerland	Pharmaceuticals
Merck & Co.	MRK	$111,610	US	Pharmaceuticals

Source: Thomson Reuters, as of 12/31/2009.

Table 1.3   Largest Companies in the Health Care Equipment &
Services Group

Name	Ticker	Market Cap ($Mil)	Country	Industry
Medtronic	MDT	$48,583	US	Health Care Equipment
Baxter International	BAX	$35,376	US	Health Care Equipment
UnitedHealth Group	UNH	$35,418	US	Managed Health Care
WellPoint	WLP	$26,717	US	Managed Health Care
Medco Health Solutions	MHS	$30,470	US	Health Care Services
Covidien	COV	$24,062	US	Health Care Equipment

Source: Thomson Reuters, as of 12/31/2009.

food, water, air, and metals. There are over 1,600 publicly traded firms globally in this segment.[2] Table 1.2 lists the largest firms in this industry group.

The Health Care Equipment & Services group includes medical equipment makers, health insurance firms (called managed health), pharmacy benefit managers, hospitals, and technology firms. There are over 1,200 globally publicly traded firms in this segment.[3] Table 1.3 lists the largest firms in this group.

HEALTH CARE CHARACTERISTICS

Although Health Care firms span various industries, firms in this sector tend to share some similar characteristics. Generally, the sector as a whole:

- Is less economically sensitive and less volatile than the broad market.
- Deals with heavy government involvement.
- Has a large, global market.
- Is mostly characterized by big cap, growth companies.
- Is dominated by US firms.

Let's look at each of these characteristics in more detail.

Less Economically Sensitive

As we'll cover more in depth in Chapter 4, Health Care's drivers can be somewhat independent of pure economic growth. In other words, demand for Health Care goods and services typically holds up well even when the economy sours. In a down economy, consumers might buy fewer Consumer Discretionary goods and firms might delay upgrading computer systems during recession (which isn't great for the Tech sector), but folks are likely to keep taking heart medication and visiting the emergency room. In other words, Health Care firms produce goods and services for which there is typically *inelastic* demand.

Health Care, as a relatively economically insensitive sector, can be a useful part of your portfolio because it can perform relatively well when the economy contracts and broader markets decline. For this reason, the sector is also sometimes described as *defensive.* This doesn't necessarily mean Health Care stocks will post positive returns during a market downturn—instead, those stocks may just perform relatively better than stocks as a whole during those periods. Nor does it mean the sector must underperform in good times. For example, Health

Elasticity

Elasticity is a measure of one variable's sensitivity to a change in another variable. The term references changes in demand relative to changes in price or income. The concept of elasticity is core to understanding what makes the Health Care sector tick.

Health Care products are generally inelastic because they are necessities purchased regardless of how an individual's personal economic situation shifts over time. Discretionary purchases, like vacations, are just the opposite—elastic—because income or price fluctuations do materially impact demand.

For example, if our friend Shane's income increased, he wouldn't demand more surgery or prescription drugs. And if the price of surgery or drugs increased, he would still need those things to keep him alive. An elastic industry might be the Consumer Discretionary industry. Take the Automobile industry, for example. An increase in either income or the price of cars could substantially alter demand.

Table 1.4   Pharmaceuticals Outperformance During US
Bear Markets

Bear Market/ Corrections	S&P 500 Pharma	S&P 500	Pharma Outperformance
1929–1932	−79.6%	−86.0%	6.5%
1934–1935	16.6%	−24.2%	40.8%
1937–1942	−46.6%	−57.7%	11.1%
1946–1948	−47.5%	−27.0%	−20.5%
1956–1957	20.9%	−19.0%	40.0%
1961–1962	−33.8%	−23.5%	−10.3%
1966	−15.0%	−17.6%	2.5%
1968–1970	−2.6%	−32.9%	30.3%
1973–1974	−34.3%	−46.2%	11.9%
1976–1978	−16.4%	−19.0%	2.6%
1980–1982	1.3%	−23.8%	25.1%
1987	−26.0%	−30.2%	4.2%
1990	−3.4%	−15.8%	12.5%
1998	−4.2%	−15.6%	11.3%
2000–2002	−26.3%	−46.3%	19.9%
2007–2009	−36.5%	−52.6%	16.0%

Source: Global Financial Data, Inc., S&P 500 Price Index, S&P 500 Pharmaceuticals Price Index, from 12/31/1925 to 12/31/2009. Performance based on monthly data.

Care led at some points as broader markets rose during the late 1990s. No sector has a single, defining driver, and there can be myriad reasons Health Care (though generally defensive in nature) might lead during broad market advances and lag during declines.

Historically, however, Health Care has held up relatively well during bear markets and corrections. Table 1.4 shows the relative performance between the S&P 500 and S&P Pharmaceuticals during bear markets going back to 1929. (Note: We encourage you to always think globally, but when studying history, US markets are a good proxy for the world because we have more and better data going back further on US stocks at this point.) Pharmaceuticals—a majority of the Health Care sector—outperformed the broader market in 14 of 16 bear markets and/or corrections—sometimes by a very wide margin.

Table 1.5   Global Health Care Outperformance During Global Bear Markets

Peak	Bottom	MSCI World Health Care	MSCI World	Health Care Outperformance
3/27/2000	10/9/2002	−14.50%	−51.40%	36.90%
10/31/2007	3/9/2009	−39.30%	−59.10%	19.80%

Source: Thomson Reuters, MSCI Inc.[4] MSCI World Index, MSCI World Health Care Price Index from 3/27/2000 to 03/09/2009. Performance based on daily data.

At this point, there's limited sector-specific data going back very far for global stocks, but what we've observed so far for the world seems to confirm the US history. Table 1.5 shows global Health Care handily outperforming global stocks over the last two bear markets.

Beta   Another way to help determine how volatile a sector is, is to look at its *beta*. Because broad markets tend to rise in anticipation of strong or ongoing economic growth and fall in anticipation of economic weakness, we can measure if a sector tends to rise or fall more or less than the market using beta. Beta is a statistical measure of relative *volatility* or sensitivity between an asset (e.g., sector, portfolio, or individual security) and a broader index such as the S&P 500 or MSCI World Index.

The index you measure against has a beta of one. If the subject (sector, portfolio, single stock) you compare it to has a number less than one, it's less sensitive than the general market; a number greater than one means it's more sensitive than the market.

Keep in mind, beta isn't static. There will be periods when a sector will have higher or lower beta during different periods. Also, beta is inherently a backward-looking measurement. Some people say beta measures risk. That's partially right—beta *measured* volatility risk. It does not tell you how volatile something will be going forward.

However, it's still a useful metric and can show us, historically over long periods, which sectors tend to have higher or lower beta than the

Table 1.6   Sector Betas to the MSCI World and S&P 500

Sector	Beta to MSCI World	Beta to S&P 500
Financials	1.38	1.57
Materials	1.35	1.28
Industrials	1.15	1.21
Information Technology	1.03	1.13
Consumer Discretionary	1.00	1.15
Energy	0.98	0.87
Telecommunication Services	0.72	0.74
Utilities	0.71	0.58
Consumer Staples	0.60	0.55
Health Care	**0.60**	**0.69**

Source: Thomson Reuters, MSCI Inc.,[5] MSCI World Price Index, S&P 500 Price Index from 12/31/1994 to 12/31/2009. MSCI World and S&P 500 Sector Price Indexes: Financials, Materials, Industrials, Information Technology, Consumer Discretionary, Energy, Telecommunications, Utilities, and Consumer Staples from 12/31/2004 to 12/31/2009.

market. Table 1.6 shows, for example, betas for the standard sectors relative to both world and US stocks from 1995 to 2009.

Health Care historically has one of the lower betas among all 10 sectors. A 0.6 beta to the MSCI World Index can be interpreted to mean that if the World Index increased 10 percent, the Health Care sector would be anticipated to increase 6 percent. Conversely Health Care is expected to only decrease 6 percent if the broader market fell 10 percent. In contrast, the more economically sensitive Materials sector has a beta of 1.35 versus the MSCI World index—so if the broader market increased 10 percent, the Materials sector would be expected to increase 13.5 percent.

This also means that a lower beta isn't inherently better than a higher beta. Lower beta sectors have historically fallen less than markets have, but they have also underperformed overall during rising periods. Both low and high beta categories play important roles in a portfolio.

EPS Comparison   Corporate earnings are a primary driver of share price performance over long periods. Therefore, we should expect earnings of a more economically sensitive sector, like Materials (for

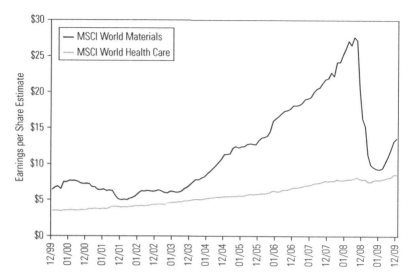

Figure 1.2   Health Care and Materials 10-Year EPS Estimates Comparison

Source: Thomson Reuters, MSCI World Health Care Index, MSCI World Materials Index from 12/31/1999 to 12/31/2009.

illustration's sake), to be more volatile than Health Care. Figure 1.2 shows earnings-per-share (EPS) estimates for both Materials and Health Care—and Materials is clearly more volatile. Starting in 2004, when that bull market was already a year old, Materials earnings started increasing sharply in erratic spurts—even into 2008. Estimates fell off sharply in the wake of the credit crisis spurred by the Lehman Brothers bankruptcy—which had a devastating impact on almost all sectors. Meanwhile, during that period, Health Care earnings estimates were slow and steady. Note, when Materials estimates dropped, they fell to the level of the Health Care estimates. Quite a roller coaster ride to end up back in the same place. That's the difference between an economically sensitive sector (Materials) and one that's less so (Health Care).

Now look at Figure 1.3. You'll see stock prices traveled a similar path as the earnings estimates—with some more volatility. It's clear from these graphs that EPS volatility helps explain quite a bit of share price volatility.

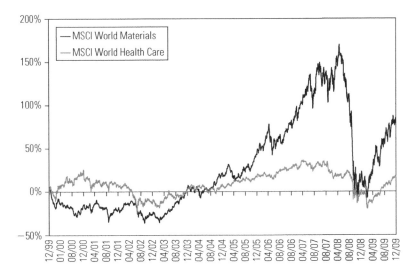

Figure 1.3   Share Price Performances of Health Care and Materials Over the Last 10 Years

Source: Thomson Reuters; MSCI, Inc.,[6] MSCI World Health Care Price Index, MSCI World Materials Price Index from 12/31/1999 to 12/31/2009.

Further, note from late 1999 to mid-2003, Health Care outperformed Materials—the market was in a state of contraction for much of that period, which coincided with recession in 2001. Then, Health Care significantly underperformed Materials starting with the next bull market, which returned in early 2003—all while Materials earnings estimates spiked and Health Care stayed steady. (Again, Health Care earnings estimates weren't lousy; they were just less rosy compared to Materials). Finally, Materials and the broader market fell while Health Care held up better during the precipitous market decline in 2008. That's pretty textbook behavior for a defensive, economically insensitive sector.

Heavy Government Involvement

Few sectors have as much heavy government involvement as Health Care—understanding the role of government and potential policy changes is vital when researching Health Care companies. In many countries, the government pays for nearly all of its citizens' medical costs. Since the government is paying the bill, expect it to be directly or indirectly mandating prices as well as what procedures and drugs will be covered.

As a major, if not the largest, net consumer of health services in many nations, governments can exert significant pricing influence. A government's decision to reduce or increase payments for certain services can have material ramifications on a firm's bottom line. Regulatory bodies can approve or reject new innovations while requiring existing products be pulled from the market. Regulators can appear to be more or less stringent at times, which can also directly impact companies' sales and profits.

Time spent understanding existing and upcoming legislation both in the US and globally is time well spent in the Health Care sector. (Health care systems of major countries are covered in Chapters 2 and 3.)

A Big, Global Market

George Carlin famously said, "I wanna live. I don't wanna die. That's the whole meaning of life: Not dying!" His words must be at least somewhat true because tremendous amounts of money are spent each year to improve or maintain people's health. Global health care spending was approximately $6 trillion in 2009, or roughly 9 percent of global gross domestic product (GDP).[7] This amount exceeds the total economic output of Japan, the world's third largest economy.[8] A $6 trillion market makes the Health Care segment one of the largest in the world. In the US alone, 2009 health care spending was projected to be $2.5 trillion, more than 17 percent of its GDP.[9] Health spending is expected to grow due to demographics, demand, and inefficiencies. Figure 1.4 shows health care spending as a percentage of GDP among major nations as of 2008, the latest available data.

Health Care is global in nature. Naturally, most everyone everywhere consumes some amount of health care. But it's also common

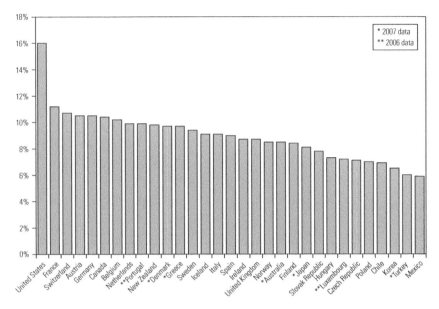

Figure 1.4   Country Health Care Expenditures as a Percentage of GDP: 2008

Source: Organisation for Economic Co-operation and Development

for firms to derive a significant portion of their revenues outside their home country. And it's becoming increasingly common for patients to seek medical attention outside their country's borders. As some nations try to restrict health care markets through regulation and price caps, some consumers can still create their own, somewhat freer markets by shopping outside their borders.

Mostly Big Cap, Growth Companies

Growth companies tend to have relatively higher valuation ratios such as price-to-earnings, price-to-book, price-to-sales, and price-to-cash flow. Value-oriented companies tend to have relatively lower valuations. Health Care firms are historically known to have more growth characteristics than value. Innovation, favorable demographics, and inelastic demand help drive profits and valuations. In contrast, Materials are generally known to have more value chacteristics

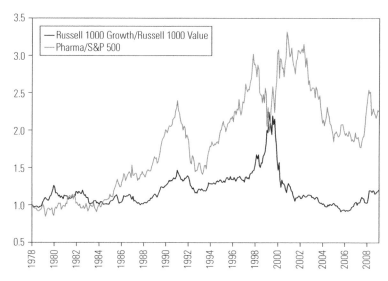

Figure 1.5   Health Care Performance When Growth Outperforms Value

Source: Global Financial Data, Inc., Thomson Reuters, Russell 2000 Growth Price Index, Russell 2000 Value Price Index, S&P 500 Pharmaceuticals Index, S&P 500 Index from 12/29/1978 to 12/31/2009.

because investors are generally not willing to pay high prices for volatile earnings cycles.

If you anticipate growth will outperform value, then perhaps it may be a good time to consider increasing exposure to the Health Care sector. Figure 1.5 shows the relationship between when Pharmaceuticals (again, our proxy for Health Care) outperforms the broader market and when growth outperforms value since 1979. The relationship is not perfect, but it is apparent. Growth outperforms value and Pharmaceuticals outperforms the S&P 500 when the lines increase, and both underperform when the lines decrease.

Big Versus Small   When it comes to size, Health Care firms are generally larger stocks market cap–wise. There are numerous small cap Health Care firms, and Biotechnology firms can be tiny, but the sector is dominated by large Pharmaceuticals (as we will see in Chapter 4). Table 1.7 provides a list showing the weighted average and the median

Table 1.7   MSCI World Sector Market Capitalizations

Sector	Weighted Average Market Cap ($Mil)	Median Market Cap ($Mil)
Energy	$106,708	$9,229
Information Technology	$94,650	$7,064
Telecommunication Services	$84,097	$10,866
Health Care	**$72,409**	**$7,515**
Consumer Staples	$69,145	$7,977
Financials	$56,556	$7,305
Materials	$37,478	$5,853
Consumer Discretionary	$31,434	$5,918
Industrials	$31,430	$5,894
Utilities	$31,260	$7,566

Source: Thomson Reuters, MSCI, Inc.[10] as of 12/31/2009.

market capitalizations of all 10 sectors. While Health Care is dwarfed by Energy, its weighted-average market cap is still sizable.

The weighted average is more useful than the median in understanding how the overall sector behaves. Though each sector has firms of varying market size, the larger firms inherently have more impact on overall sector performance. So while the median market cap might be much smaller, the overall sector will behave, by and large, like a firm with a weighted-average market cap.

Mostly US

The US is home to the majority of the world's Health Care market cap—largely because it's the world's largest market and known to have the most innovative health care sources. Part of the reason the US dominates Health Care is because Americans spend the most and demand the newest medical innovations, allowing corporations to further research and development (R&D) expenditures. Others argue America is the leader in Health Care because its capitalistic system rewards innovation. (And we'd agree.) Table 1.8 shows Health Care firms' market capitalization by country. The United States is by far the dominant player in Health Care.

Table 1.8   MSCI ACWI Health Care Exposure by Country

Country	% of MSCI ACWI Health Care
US	59.8%
Switzerland	11.1%
UK	8.3%
Japan	5.5%
France	4.0%
Germany	3.8%
Israel	2.5%
Denmark	1.9%
Australia	1.2%
India	0.4%
South Africa	0.2%
Sweden	0.2%
Belgium	0.2%
Ireland	0.2%
Hungary	0.1%
Canada	0.1%
Korea	0.1%
Russia	0.1%
China	0.1%
Finland	0.1%
Spain	0.1%

Source: Thomson Reuters; MSCI, Inc.[11] as of 12/31/2009.

Chapter Recap

You've now been introduced to some of the fundamental characteristics distinguishing the Health Care sector. We will build upon many of this chapter's concepts as we progress.

- The sector is composed of two main segments—Pharmaceuticals, Biotechnology & Life Sciences and Health Care Equipment & Services.
- Government is heavily involved in the Health Care industry.
- The US is the only developed country not to offer health care to all citizens.
- The Health Care market is one of the largest markets in the world.
- The sector is known to have defensive, large cap, and growth characteristics.
- The US dominates the market.

THE US HEALTH CARE SYSTEM

Before understanding a game's players, you must understand how the game is played. Therefore, Chapters 2 and 3 discuss how Health Care systems operate in different nations—and there are vital differences.

Much of this chapter concentrates on the US system, the world's largest Health Care market, and centers on insurance coverage and the various types of insurance plans—which can lend some clarity around how many of the Health Care firms you may invest in garner income.

Health Care economics is so complex, a whole book could be dedicated to the subject alone—and it would be lengthy. This book does not try to cover all the complexities or solve them. It does, however, attempt to help the reader obtain a high-level understanding of the framework in which the industry operates and provide a few basic examples.

The goal of this chapter is to cover:

- Costs and funding mechanisms
- How the system operates
- The regulatory system

WHY DOES IT COST SO MUCH?

One of the most important questions in Health Care is: Who pays for what? Health Care expenditures were roughly $2.5 trillion in 2009, about 17 percent of US GDP—making the US health care market the world's largest. Expenses are shared between the government, insurance firms, and individuals. The *private* industry (i.e., not government), namely insurance companies and individuals, pays for more than half of all health costs. Table 2.1 shows US health expenditures by source of funds. Table 2.2 shows where that money goes. Over half of expenditures are hospital and doctor care.

Distorted Supply and Unstoppable Demand

As this book is written in 2009 and 2010, health care is a topic of much debate. But no matter where you stand, most people agree health care costs a lot—for governments, employers, and individuals. But why? Simple—in the US, demand exceeds supply. Add that to vast structural inefficiencies. For example, every year, billions are likely lost to Medicare fraud, simply because the structure is flawed.

It may seem counterintuitive at first, but health care is a service, just like any other. But where health care differs from other services—tax accounting, banking, home decorating, you name it—is how services are paid. Health care is perhaps the only service where

Table 2.1   2008 US Health Care Spending by Source of Funds

Source of Funds	% of Total Spending
Private Insurance	33%
Out of Pocket	12%
Other	8%
Total Private	**53%**
Federal	35%
State & Local	12%
Total Government	**47%**

Source: Centers for Medicare & Medicaid Services, "National Health Expenditures Aggregate" (page 3).

Table 2.2   2008 US Health Care Expenditures

Source Expenditures	% of Health Spending
Hospital Care	31%
Physician and Clinical Services	21%
Prescription Drugs	10%
Administration and Net Cost of Private Health Insurance	7%
Nursing Home Care	6%
Structures and Equipment	5%
Dental Services	4%
Other Personal Health Care	3%
Public Health Activity	3%
Other Professional Services	3%
Home Health Care	3%
Research	2%
Other Nondurable Medical Products	2%
Durable Medical Equipment	1%

Source: Centers for Medicare & Medicaid Services, "National Health Expenditures Aggregate" (page 2).

a wholly unrelated third party pays the bills, most of the time. You receive service, the doctor delivers it. You take pharmaceuticals, a drug firm makes them. You use a heart monitor, a device firm manufactures it. But most of the time, doctors, pharmacies, and so on, are paid by insurance firms or the government, not the patient receiving the care.

Health care supply can be thought about in a number of ways. First, it's unlikely a million new doctors enter the market next year, tied to the time and cost involved in becoming a doctor. Further, health care innovations are a long time in coming—pharmaceuticals, devices, and even procedures go through long rounds of rigorous testing. So, in that sense, you don't need to wrangle with the price impact of a flood of new supply. On the other hand, health care access is restricted, distorted, or both to varying degrees by those third parties—governments and insurance firms. How much supply is distorted depends on each nation's delivery system—and there's not much to be done about those supply issues. Short of a major systemic overhaul (which, as the US learned in 2009, doesn't happen fast or easily), the supply side is relatively more stable in the short run. But constricted or distorted supply is certainly one major factor in keeping Health Care costs high and rising.

Demand Drivers

The other side of the equation is demand for health care services, and in the US, demand just keeps rising—and so do prices. There's no single party responsible—everyone involved in the process including the patient, provider, and payer contributes to rising costs. The primary demand drivers are:

- Imperfect information
- Asymmetry
- Preventable diseases
- Defensive medicine
- External demand

Imperfect Information   Most people wouldn't buy a car, a TV, or even a steak dinner without knowing the price ahead of time. But health care is unique—many times, patients don't even know what a product or service costs, either before or after it's been provided. Because services are usually paid for by someone else, individuals have limited (or no) incentives to ensure they get the best bang for their buck. You probably do extensive research and shop around before buying a car, and you might not return to a restaurant you feel overcharged you. But why should you shop for the best price when you aren't paying?

People generally want more of something at a lower price and less of something at higher prices. Because health care is usually paid for or subsidized by a third party, it *feels* cheap or even free, even when it's not—which can lead to almost unlimited demand. This is one reason countries with socialized medicine must ration care—it's the only way to keep costs in check. Plus, in many instances, they simply don't have enough personnel to meet the demand. All this contributes to higher prices.

Additionally, though the US is frequently criticized for not having a public health system, no patients are turned away at emergency rooms. For the 15 percent of the US population who are under- or uninsured, service received through ERs can indeed be free. But hospitals must recoup those costs by cost shifting and charging those with insurance—private or government-provided.

Asymmetry   Due to a lack of transparency, health care is unique in that providers have far more knowledge than their customers about products and pricing (called asymmetric information). Sometimes doctors are paid on a "fee-for-service" basis, meaning they collect revenue for each office visit, test, or service provided. Fee-for-service could be seen as providing doctors incentives to schedule unnecessary appointments or tests. Some of that could be driven by *defensive medicine* (described in a moment)—where doctors order excessive tests to limit their liability. But because providers know the costs and the patient doesn't (and likely isn't paying for it anyway), there can be incentive to sell more products and services than is necessary.

Preventable Diseases   Preventable diseases, like those related to smoking and obesity, are large drivers of health costs. Annual wasted health care spending in the US is estimated to be up to $1.2 trillion per year, with preventable diseases or risky lifestyles costing nearly $500 billion.[1]

Defensive Medicine   In the US, doctors are frequent targets of litigation—even very good doctors are frequently sued, rightly or wrongly. Doctors wanting to avoid excessive lawsuits may resort to scheduling excessive tests or procedures. These actions may not be in the patient's best interest but are the result of doctors attempting to limit liability. And it can be costly. In fact, defensive medicine is one of the largest components of wasteful spending—costing at least $210 billion per year.[2]

Can Insurance Costs Reduce the Supply of Doctors?

Malpractice insurance, like any other insurance, is largely priced based on risks associated with potential loss tied to the probability of loss. Medical malpractice premiums vary by state and type of medical practice, with the higher risk medical professions incurring higher insurance premiums. Obstetricians, gynecologists (OB/GYNs), and anesthesiologists are high risk professions *where premiums exceeding $200,000 per year are normal.* These are significant costs for small businesses.

And make no mistake, doctors' offices are mostly small businesses. A medical practice operates like any other business, and a primary goal is to maximize profits. Profits decline if owners/managers cannot pass on enough costs to customers, and they may be forced to relocate to lower cost areas. This is happening in traditionally higher cost states like Florida and Illinois, where increasing medical malpractice insurance premiums have driven some doctors to relocate to different states (or counties within states) and limit the types of services provided, and also possibly prevented new doctors from entering the business. Malpractice insurance costs can reduce the supply of doctors or services. Stable demand and a reduced supply of doctors generally drive overall health care costs higher.

External Demand The US market isn't impacted by just US demand, but frequently demand from the whole world. In many ways, the US private Health Care market subsidizes the rest of world. This is because governments (including the US government—most other nations buy our pharmaceuticals and devices) force private firms to accept price caps. In other words, the private sector must overcharge US patients where a somewhat freer market exists in order to recoup slimmer margins or suffer outright losses from selling into nations with price caps; therefore, undercharging some while overcharging others leads to pricing distortions.

It's impossible to measure how much certain supply and demand distortions contribute to higher costs, but Table 2.3 shows some measurable waste contributors. "Poor lifestyle" (e.g., preventable diseases related to obesity, smoking, ignoring doctor's orders, etc.) is estimated to cost a whopping $500 billion annually. Defensive medicine costs at

Table 2.3   Sources of Excessive US Health Care Spending

Source	Estimated Annual Wasted Spending
Defensive Medicine	$210 billion
Inefficient Claims Processing	Up to $210 billion
Obesity	$200 billion
Smoking	Up to $191 billion
Ignoring Doctor's Orders	$100 billion
Ineffective Use of Information Technology	Up to $88 billion

Source: PriceWaterhouseCoopers, "The Price of Excess: Identifying Waste in Healthcare Spending" (accessed August 27, 2010).

least $210 billion a year. Inefficient claims processing is where a lot of fraud happens, but it's also waste tied to navigating the bureaucracy of insurance firms—public and private.

PRIVATE VERSUS PUBLIC

The US is the only major developed nation without some sort of universal health care. However, the government is still significantly involved because it pays for a massive amount of health costs, sets regulations, and oversees health care policy. US citizens and politicians constantly battle to determine if health care should be provided by the government or if the private markets would make the system more efficient.

Note: The purpose of this book isn't to make policy comments, but to arm readers with tools to determine when various Health Care industries are likely to perform relatively better or worse than broader markets. Whether a health care system is wholly free or increasingly government run, there will be times when Health Care stocks are more or less attractive.

US citizens can get insurance through the government and/or private firms. About 65 percent of people under age 65 get private health insurance from a private insurance firm contracted through their employer (which may be completely or partially employer-subsidized),[3] while nearly everyone age 65 and older, the poor, and disabled can get insurance through the government.

About 15 percent of the US population is uninsured[4]—though even this number is debatable. Many individuals counted as uninsured may be uninsured only temporarily because they are between jobs, changing insurance providers, or just rolling off of their parents' plans, for example. However, federal law requires hospitals and doctors treat emergency patients regardless of ability to pay.

Types of Private Health Insurance Plans

Private health insurance providers may either be for-profit or not-for-profit entities. Additionally, insurance plans are typically either *fee-for-service* (indemnity plans) or *managed care*. Fee-for-service plans pay health providers for each service, and patients pay a portion of the bill. Managed care attempts to manage health costs by arranging a network of health providers at discounted rates and, in exchange, the providers get a larger customer base. Managed care patients typically pay just a co-pay, though they are sometimes responsible for a portion of the bill, depending on how the plan is structured. (Note: Not all managed care plans are private. For example, Medicare is a managed care plan but is government-run.)

Private insurance plan types include:

- Health maintenance organizations (HMO)
- Preferred provider organizations (PPO)
- Point of service (POS)
- Consumer-directed plans

Health Maintenance Organizations   HMOs are a relatively restrictive type of insurance plan in which a patient selects a primary care physician from within the designated network. That doctor can then refer the patient to specialists if needed. Excluding emergencies, services are not generally covered if the patient uses an out-of-network physician, which can limit patient choices.

Because of limits and restrictions, these plans are generally the least expensive for patients and require minimal co-payments (normally about $20 to $40) and deductibles. HMOs often have *capitated contracts* with providers, under which they pay a fixed monthly fee for services, regardless of how often a patient sees the doctor.

Preferred Provider Organizations   PPOs allow members to select doctors in or out of network, but fees are higher for out-of-network doctors. PPOs adhere to payment contracts and use procedure protocols designed by plan administrators. Instead of the nominal co-pay patients have under a HMO, PPOs generally have a deductible and coinsurance. For example, a patient may have a $500 deductible and 80 percent/20 percent coinsurance—the patient pays the first $500 of expenses plus 20 percent of the remaining bill, which is usually subject to a maximum out-of-pocket expense.

Point of Service   POS plans are hybrids of HMOs and PPOs in which a network primary care physician is chosen as the point-of-service contact, and the doctor may refer the patient to out-of-network specialists. Out-of-network doctors come at higher fees to patients.

Consumer-Directed Plans   Consumer-directed plans have increased in popularity as a way to control health care costs. These plans are usually high deductible plans, where the patient is responsible for the first few thousand dollars of health care expenses. Ideally, the more "skin" patients have in the game, the more conscientious they'll be about costs. High deductible plans may come with savings and tax advantages to the patient.

For example, patients can open high deductible *health savings accounts* (HSA) that allow them to save a predetermined amount each year (say $2,500), pretax. These funds grow tax deferred (i.e., investment income and gains are not taxed each year). When a patient has a medical claim, he may be responsible for the first few thousand dollars of expenses—this is his deductible. The patient then pays for the expenses with funds from the HSA. Any amount withdrawn from the HSA and spent on qualified medical expenses isn't subject to income taxes. The thinking behind HSAs is patients will be more cost conscious because they're responsible for the first chunk of expenses.

Types of Government Health Insurance Plans

Government programs also come in a variety of stripes. Although these various programs are funded by the government, coordination and administration are often outsourced to private health insurers. The plan types include:

- Medicare
- Medicare Advantage
- Medicaid
- Veterans Health Administration (VHA)
- Military Health System/TRICARE
- State Children's Health Insurance Program (SCHIP)

Medicare   In 1965, President Lyndon B. Johnson signed into law the Social Security Act of 1965, which established *Medicare*, a socialized health insurance program mainly for disabled persons and people aged 65 and over. Medicare is generally financed by payroll taxes, general revenues, member premiums, and taxes on Social Security benefits. With approximately 45 million members, Medicare is the largest payer for medical care in the US, with expenditures totaling over $460 billion in 2008.[5]

Medicare offers several benefits on a fee-for-service basis: Part A covers inpatient hospital stays (at least one night) and doctor's expenses. Part B covers outpatient costs like doctor's visits, tests, and equipment. Part C is Medicare Advantage (see next section). Part D is a prescription drug plan (PDP) that went into effect January 2006. (Part D is regulated by Medicare but administered by the private health insurance industry.) Parts C and D became industry growth drivers as more insured individuals demanded more health care products and services.

Medicare Advantage   Medicare Advantage (MA) is a relatively new program. Launched in 2003, it's Medicare with extra benefits administered through private health insurers. Medicare (through the Center for Medicare and Medicaid Services, or CMS) pays private health insurers a set amount (capitated rate) for each member per period, known as reimbursements. MA plans are required by law to offer benefits on par with traditional Medicare. The government currently pays MA programs higher rates than it would cost Medicare. It does so to entice private industry into the market. MA providers use the excess reimbursements to offer extra benefits such as dental, vision, and gym memberships. MA plans can take the form of HMOs, PPOs, fee-for-service, and high deductible plans.

In 2006, Medicare began to reimburse plans under a bidding process. If a plan's bid is higher than the benchmark, the member pays the difference via a monthly premium. A company bidding below the benchmark gets 75 percent of the savings, while Medicare gets 25 percent. The 75 percent savings goes back to the member in the form of more benefits.

Medicaid The Social Security Act of 1965 also established Medicaid, a socialized health insurance program funded by both the federal government and state government to provide health care benefits to low income people. Total Medicaid expenditures were over $340 billion per year in 2008 and covered more than 50 million members.[6] Nearly 60 percent is funded by the federal government,[7] but Medicaid is managed by the states. State participation is optional, but since 1982, all states offer Medicaid. Unlike Medicare, Medicaid does not have a dedicated trust fund to pay for costs. Instead, expenses are funded from general revenues on an as-needed basis. Private health insurers often administer the program.

Veterans Health Administration (VHA) Dating back to the late 1700s, the VHA provides health care benefits to US veterans, particularly for those injured during service. It covers approximately 8 million members and has an annual budget surpassing $40 billion.[8] It operates hospitals, clinics, nursing homes, and counseling centers across the US. The VHA is known to have one of the most advanced medical records systems in the country, employing technology to reduce medical errors and costs.

Military Health System/TRICARE This program provides health care coverage to military personnel, military retirees, and their dependants. Its 2010 annual budget is $47 billion and covers approximately 10 million members located in the US and abroad.[9] TRICARE is broken down into 12 regions within the US and offers various types of insurance programs similar to private insurance. It also comes with various co-payments and coinsurance amounts.

State Children's Health Insurance Program (SCHIP) Created in 1997, SCHIP is a state-administered program (with federal funding support) designed to provide health insurance coverage to uninsured children. This is specifically for children (and some qualifying parents) whose families have low incomes but not low enough to qualify for Medicaid. The program covers approximately 11 million children and fewer than 1 million adults.[10] In 2009, President Barack Obama signed legislation increasing the SCHIP budget to nearly $60 billion over five years, funded by taxes on tobacco. This will expand the SCHIP program to more children.

THE REGULATORY SYSTEM

In health care, regulation is a constant fact of life. Regulation is jointly carried out by the state and federal governments. The US Department of Health and Human Services (HHS) is a cabinet-level organization responsible for health care regulation and providing health care to the less fortunate. Its work is carried out by 13 agencies:

1. The Office of the Secretary (OS)
2. Administration for Children and Families (ACF)
3. Administration on Aging (AoA)
4. Agency for Healthcare Research and Quality (AHRQ)
5. Agency for Toxic Substances and Disease Registry (ATSDR)
6. Centers for Disease Control and Prevention (CDC)
7. Centers for Medicare and Medicaid Services (CMS)

8. Food and Drug Administration (FDA)
9. Health Resources and Services Administration (HRSA)
10. Indian Health Service (IHS)
11. National Institutes of Health (NIH)
12. Office of Inspector General (OIG)
13. Substance Abuse and Mental Health Services Administration (SAMHSA)

From an investment management standpoint, the FDA, CMS, and NIH are agencies you will hear about more often.

Legislative Players

Health care legislation typically springs from some key congressional committees, including:

Senate

- Health, Education, Labor, and Pensions Committee (www.help.senate.gov) has jurisdiction over public health and medical research.
- Finance Committee (www.finance.senate.gov) has jurisdiction over Medicare, Medicaid, and other programs financed by specific taxes or trusts.

House

- Energy and Commerce Committee (www.energycommerce.house.gov) has jurisdiction over public health and food and drug safety.
- Ways and Means Committee (www.waysandmeans.house.gov) has jurisdiction over Medicare.
- Education and Labor Committee (www.edlabor.house.gov) has jurisdiction over employer/employee relations like access to health care, worker's compensation, and medical leave.

Following these committees is a good way to watch for legislative developments that can, at times, have serious impacts on various Health Care industries earnings. However, keep in mind that proposed bills can materially change or fail altogether during the legislative process.

Food and Drug Administration (FDA)   The FDA is responsible for protecting, regulating, and supervising human and veterinary drugs, medical equipment, the food supply, cosmetics, dietary supplements, and products emitting radiation. Regulation covers product safety, efficacy, manufacturing, and marketing. This is the agency that determines if a drug/equipment company's product is approved or removed from the market. Therefore, the FDA is a powerful force that can help determine a firm's success or failure. See Chapter 5 for more information on the drug/equipment approval process.

Centers for Medicare and Medicaid Services (CMS)   CMS is responsible for administering Medicare and working in conjunction with states to administer Medicaid and the State Children's Health Insurance Program (SCHIP). CMS also provides a lot of useful information and statistics on health care spending and other types of data. This is the agency that determines how much the government will pay for medical products and services, and because the government is the largest payer for medical services, CMS can have a material impact on Health Care companies' revenues and profits.

National Institutes of Health (NIH)   The NIH conducts and supports medical research. It has a staff of scientists and provides grants to researchers at universities, medical schools, and other research institutions. The agency spends nearly $30 billion per year and supports thousands of research projects. The NIH and its budget can have a material impact on research companies' revenues and profits.

US HEALTH CARE REFORM

After a tumultuous year-long debate, in March 2010, President Barack Obama signed the largest health care legislative measure since the introduction of Medicare in 1965. The new law is expected to expand insurance coverage to 32 million uninsured Americans and cost roughly $950 billion over 10 years. Various parts of the legislation will be enacted over several years. The new program will be funded with cuts to Medicare spending, from fees on drug makers, medical equipment manufacturers, and health insurance companies, tax hikes on the wealthy, and other various fees.

A whole book could be written on this legislative change, but for this book, the goal is to help you understand what the new legislation is and encourage you to start thinking about how it could impact all the various industries. Table 2.4 is an overview of reform highlights and a timeline showing when those changes will be implemented. Of particular note are key changes such as:

- Insurers are barred from denying coverage based on pre-existing conditions
- Insurers can no longer have lifetime benefit limits on coverage
- Insurers must spend 85 percent of premiums on medical benefits for large group plans and 80 percent for small group and individual plans (see Chapter 5 for a discussion on minimum loss ratios)
- Establishes new state-based insurance exchanges where customers can shop for insurance policies
- Requires individuals to buy insurance and employers to offer insurance or be subject to fines
- Expands Medicaid coverage and federal subsidies for individuals to obtain insurance

Table 2.4 Overview of New Health Care Legislative Changes

Year	Taxes & Fees	Benefits	Other
2010	10% tax on indoor tanning salon services.	Establishes temporary high-risk insurance pool to cover individuals with pre-existing conditions. Subsidies for small businesses to provide coverage to employees. Insurers barred from denying coverage to children based on pre-existing conditions. Children allowed to stay on parents' insurance until age 26.	Authorizes FDA to approve generic biologic drugs and grant biologics 12 years of exclusive use before generics can be developed.
2011	Drug makers face annual fee of $2.5 billion (rises in subsequent years to $4.2 billion in 2018, and then lowers to $2.8 billion for 2019 and beyond). Exclude costs for nonprescribed over-the-counter drugs from being reimbursed through health savings accounts. Increase tax to 20% of the disbursed amount on distributions from health savings accounts not used for qualified medical expenses.	Set up long-term care program under which people pay premiums into system for at least five years and become eligible for support payments if they need assistance in daily living. Pharmaceutical manufacturers to provide a 50% discount on brand-name drugs to fill in the Medicare Part D coverage gap (effective 2011–2015).	NA
2012	NA	NA	NA
2013	New Medicare taxes on individuals earning more than $200,000 a year and couples filing jointly earning more than $250,000 a year. Tax on wages rises to 2.35% from 1.45%. New 3.8% tax on unearned income such as capital gains, dividends, and interest. Excise tax of 2.3% imposed on medical device sales. Increase threshold for medical expense itemized deductions from 7.5% of adjusted gross income to 10%. Eliminate the tax deduction for employers who receive Medicare Part D drug subsidies. Limit contributions to flexible medical savings accounts to $2,500 per year.	Create the Consumer Operated and Oriented Plan (CO-OP) program to foster the creation of nonprofit, member-run health insurance companies. Begin phasing in federal subsidies for Medicare Part D brand name prescription drugs (up to 25% in 2020, in addition to the 50% brand name manufacturer discounts).	Medicare pilot program begins to test bundled payments for care in a bid to pay for quality rather than quantity of services.

2014	Employers with more than 50 employees that don't provide affordable coverage must pay a fine if employees receive tax credits to buy insurance. Fine is up to $3,000 per employee, excluding first 30 employees. Insurance industry must pay annual fee of $8 billion (rises in subsequent years to $14 billion by 2018). Penalty for those who don't carry coverage rises to $95 or 1% of taxable income, whichever is higher.	Create state-based exchanges where uninsured individuals and small businesses can shop for coverage. Limit any waiting periods for coverage to 90 days. Insurance companies barred from denying coverage to anyone with pre-existing illness. Requirement begins for most people to have health insurance. Subsidies begin for lower and middle-income people. People at 133% of federal poverty level pay maximum of 3% of income for coverage. People at 400% of poverty level pay up to 9.5% of income. (Poverty level currently is about $22,000 for a family of four.) Medicaid expands to all Americans with income up to 133% of federal poverty level. Subsidies for small businesses to provide coverage increase. Businesses with 10 or fewer employees and average annual wages of less than $25,000 receive tax credit of up to 50% of employer's contribution. Tax credits phase out for larger businesses.	Independent Medicare board must begin to submit recommendations to curb Medicare spending if costs are rising faster than inflation.
2015	Penalty for those who don't carry coverage rises to $325 or 2% of taxable income, whichever is higher.	NA	NA
2016	Penalty for those who don't carry coverage rises to $695 or 2.5% of taxable income, whichever is greater.	NA	NA
2017	NA	Businesses with more than 100 employees can buy coverage on insurance exchanges if state permits it.	NA
2018	Excise tax of 40% imposed on health plans valued at more than $10,200 for individual coverage and $27,500 for family coverage.	NA	NA

Source: Wall Street Journal.[11]

Chapter Recap

Chapter 2 provided an introduction to the US health care system. Specifically, the chapter addressed how the system is funded, how it operates, and how it's regulated. Understanding these topics is key to understanding how health care companies operate within the context of the US system.

Keypoints

- The US Health Care market is the largest in the world with expenditures of roughly $2.5 trillion per year (approximately 17 percent of GDP) and growing.
- The US is unique in that it is the only major developed country not to have a universal health care system—US health care is funded by both the private and public sector.
- Health care expenses are directed toward many categories, with about half going toward hospitals and physicians.
- The system is littered with wasted spending.
- Private insurance plans include HMOs, PPOs, POS, and consumer-directed plans.
- Public insurance plans include Medicare, Medicaid, TRICARE, veterans insurance, and state children's plans.
- The health care system is heavily regulated, and legislative changes can materially impact health care companies' operations.
- Recent health care reform will expand coverage to many uninsured citizens, increase costs, and be implemented over several years.

3

BRIEF OVERVIEW OF HEALTH CARE SYSTEMS BY MAJOR COUNTRIES

Chapter 2 provided a basic understanding of the US health care system. The US is a massive Health Care market and a huge single economy, but half of Health Care's market is outside the US. To successfully understand where the overall sector is headed, an understanding of the global market is vital.

The largest individual Health Care markets after the US are Japan, Germany, France, United Kingdom, and China. (Note: All of these have a universal health care system of some sort, except China, which is committed to having a fully universal system by 2020.)[1] This doesn't make their health care systems superior to that of the US. Instead, it means that any Health Care analysis must take into account additional government intervention in these nations' industries and stocks.

A quick word about "universal" health care coverage. The term loosely means that all residents have access to health care coverage. Beyond that, universal systems vary greatly. In some nations, the government runs the health care system outright and operates hospitals, clinics, and so on. Some universal systems are "single-payer"—the government pays for health care whether it's delivered through a private system, a public system, or one in which public and private compete. In other nations, governments provide a public insurance option and also heavily subsidizes coverage through private plans. And though private insurance firms can exist in a universal system, they typically come under heavy government regulation. A universal system can also be a complex blend where some citizens get single-payer, some are covered privately, some get services through public facilities, and some can choose private. "Universal" isn't synonymous with "government-run," but it is synonymous with "deep government involvement."

We'll look at each of these markets, with the goal of understanding:

- Costs and financing
- How residents get coverage
- How patients get medical care
- The local regulatory system

This chapter provides a functioning overview, but if you seek additional information, Kaiser (www.kaiseredu.org), International Society for Pharmacoeconomics, the World Health Organization, and the Organisation for Economic Development are just a few places providing additional data.

JAPAN

Japan mandates universal health care coverage for all residents, mostly through employer-provided insurance plans. It's the world's third largest economy and second largest health care market—spending was roughly $400 billion per year on health care as of 2009.[2] Japan is often credited with having one of the world's longest life expectancies and lowest infant mortality rates while spending relatively less per GDP than other countries. However, the system has its share of challenges—among them, rising costs amid an aging population and long hospital waiting times.

Costs and Financing

Though Japan is the second largest Health Care market, expenditures are only about 8 percent of GDP[3]—among the lowest of major peers. Similar to the US, Japan's health care is financed by both government and private payers. However, the government pays roughly 80 percent of costs—much more than in the US—with corporate and private funding responsible for the rest.[4]

Public insurance funding comes from an approximately 8 percent payroll tax. That cost is shared by the employer and employee.[5] In addition, patients pay a co-payment up to 30 percent of costs, subject to an out-of-pocket cap.[6]

The government determines a standardized reimbursement schedule on a fee-for-service basis. The fee schedule is identical for inpatient and outpatient services. Japan also has a cultural bias against invasive surgery and therefore provides lower reimbursement levels for those procedures. The identical fee schedule and the bias against invasive surgery help tip the balance toward more outpatient procedures relative to inpatient and help reduce costs. The government reimbursement schedule covers thousands of products and services and is adjusted every two years.

How Residents Get Coverage

Thousands of health insurers operate in Japan, but they can all be generally classified into one of three categories:

1. Employer-based
2. National health plans
3. Insurance for the elderly

Employer-based plans provide coverage to company employees and their families—and this represents the bulk of Japan's insurance coverage. Premiums are set at a fixed rate by the government and split between the employer and employee. Employees are responsible for co-insurance costs of up to 30 percent of expenses. Larger firms essentially self fund their plans and may participate in *society managed plans,* which are industry-based pools. Employers and employees in larger firms typically fund the plan with no government assistance.

Small- and medium-sized firms typically enroll in a government-subsidized plan. Retirees, farmers, the unemployed, the self-employed, and others who can't qualify for employer coverage are also covered by a subsidized national plan. The elderly and disabled are covered through contributions from the other government programs, and they typically have lower co-payments, usually around 10 percent.

The various health insurance plans all offer similar benefits. The plans cover physician and hospital care, dental, and prescription drugs. Insurance plans don't cover preventative medicine (like regular annual checkups) or pregnancy, but preventative care services are provided by the public health system, and pregnancy costs are reimbursed by the government.

How Patients Get Medical Care

Unlike what most US patients would experience, Japanese patients typically don't schedule appointments. They simply show up at the doctor's office whenever they choose. Also, unlike with most US plans, patients can go to any doctor or hospital they wish, and referrals to see specialists are not required. There they don't wrangle with in-network, out-of-network issues familiar to most Americans.

Most hospitals and clinics are privately operated, but all hospitals and physician offices are nonprofit.[7] Hospitals don't compete on price because they're reimbursed the same way. Instead, they compete on technology offered and are reimbursed on a fee-for-service basis. (Remember, a fee-for-service reimbursement schedule can encourage high patient turnover because providers are paid for each visit.)

Patients have the freedom to see any doctor they wish, but the country has a shortage of physicians (about one-third fewer than the average number per 1,000 population of other OECD nations), partially due to the government's policy of limiting the number of medical students. This shortage and long waiting times make it relatively difficult for patients to be admitted into hospitals. For example, in 2007, over 14,000 emergency room patients were denied treatment at least three times by hospitals before getting help.[8] Once admitted, however, the length of stay tends to be relatively longer.

Regulatory System

The Ministry of Health, Labour, and Welfare regulates Japan's Health Care industry. Under the Ministry of Health, the Pharmaceutical and Medical Devices Agency (PMDA) reviews new drug/device applications and issues approval guidance to the Ministry of Health. Although the Ministry of Health has final authority to approve products, it generally follows PMDA's recommendation.

Relative to other developed nations, the approval process for drugs and equipment is more onerous. For example, the average length of a clinical study in Japan is 4 years, compared with 18 months in the US and UK and 30 months in France. Additionally, foreign drug manufacturers must conduct clinical trials in Japan even if the drug is approved in other countries. Even after clinical trials are finished, the final approval process is generally longer than other countries, with a median drug and equipment approval time of nearly two years. Recognizing that this is problematic, Japan is trying to bring its guidelines more in line with the US and European Union (EU) by hiring more people, consolidating government departments, and streamlining processes.

Getting a drug approved is onerous, but even once it's approved, a foreign firm can't simply sell a drug or product in Japan. Foreign firms wishing to sell a health care product must be approved as a Market Authorization Holder (MAH). They can either create an MAH-certified Japanese subsidiary or outsource to a registered MAH already doing business in Japan. Though manufacturing can be outsourced, the MAH is responsible for product safety. And the foreign firm's manufacturing facility must still be approved.

GERMANY

Dating back to the late 1800s, Germany operates Europe's oldest universal health care system in which virtually everyone is required to have health insurance. Similar to the US and Japan, Germany provides the majority of health care coverage through the employer system. However, unlike Japan, Germany's health care system isn't government run and operated—though it's heavily government subsidized. Instead, it's run by regional and national self-governing associations of payers and providers called "sickness funds," which are financed by payroll taxes. Though Germany's federal government doesn't explicitly run the health care system, it is very heavily involved in myriad ways because, in effect, it pays for it and doles out money to the various sickness funds.

Germany is the world's fourth largest economy and the third largest Health Care market. Ninety percent of Germans have some kind of government-subsidized insurance, and the private health system is small. The country is dealing with rising health costs, causing the government to scale back benefits amid budget constraints. Moreover, the bureaucratic nature of the system may help explain why the country has relatively less access to modern technology and doctors are typically considered to provide only the minimum care required.

Costs and Financing

In 2009, Germany spent roughly $360 billion annually on health care—about 10 percent of its GDP.[9] The government funds about 75 percent of total costs, and private funds cover the rest.[10] The insurance system is funded by a payroll tax of around 15 percent of earnings, which is split between employer and employee.[11] Additionally, general tax revenues finance capital and rehabilitation expenditures. Sickness funds are financially and organizationally independent of each other and are supposed to be self supportive, but budget deficits occur. The funds negotiate reimbursement contracts with regional physicians and medical companies.

How Residents Get Coverage

Germans receive coverage one of two ways:

1. Sickness funds
2. Private insurance

Sickness Funds Germans with incomes under €46,300 (approximately $66,000, as of 12/31/2009) join a statutory sickness fund. All open funds (or plans) must accept anyone who applies, regardless of health history. Employers can choose from hundreds of sickness funds and provide employees with various funds to choose from. Each fund may have different expenses based on the health of its members. The largest fund is called the Allgemeine Ortskrankenkasse, or AOK, and covers about 34 percent of the insured population.[12] Some members can choose a plan, though occupation and where a participant resides may play a big role in which plan (or plans) an individual can choose from. Although tax revenues flow into one central fund, the government doles out money to each fund based on its unique health profile.

Sickness funds cover roughly 90 percent of the population, including the unemployed, while private insurance covers most of the rest. Less than 1 percent of the population is uninsured. Only higher income earners may opt out of sickness funds and buy private insurance, but most higher income earners choose to remain in a sickness fund.

Sickness funds provide standard benefits like doctor and hospital costs, diagnostics tests, prescription drugs, and some dental work. Benefits also pay for sick leave, ranging from 70 percent to 90 percent of the patient's pay for nearly 18 months. Costs have been rising, so the government has been reducing benefits and instituting patient co-pays ranging from €10 (approximately $15) for doctor visits to a percentage of some prescription drugs.

Private Insurance Private insurance premiums are paid by both the individual and the employer. Private German plans are unique because premiums are set at the time of enrollment based on age and health status of the enrollee, similar to the US. Unlike the US, however, premiums are not adjusted for age or health status as time goes on. In German private plans, premiums increase only in relation to overall increases in health care costs. Private insurance generally offers the same coverage plus some additional benefits and services, like quicker appointments and private hospital rooms.

How Residents Get Medical Care

Similar to Japan's system, Germans are free to choose doctors, specialists, and hospitals without referrals. However, many residents have a single primary care doctor. Patients don't need to schedule appointments to see their doctor—waiting times to see a doctor are considered short.

Hospitals are a mix of government-run, nonprofit, and for-profit organizations. Hospital doctors are salaried hospital employees. Hospitals generally provide few outpatient services—most of those services are provided by clinics and office-based doctors. Office-based physicians are generally self-employed and reimbursed on a fee-for-service basis. Doctors found abusing the fee-for-service system may be fined or otherwise penalized.

Relative to other nations, Germany has a higher number of physicians per capita. This is because university expenses are cheap (i.e., government-subsidized), and students meeting certain academic requirements are guaranteed the right to study medicine. However, a large supply of doctors coupled with strict government budgets results in relatively lower physician wages. Some argue budget and salary restraints create incentives for doctors to only provide the necessary minimum care. Budget restraints also limit the amount of modern technology in the country, with the number of magnetic resonance imaging (MRI) units (7.1 per million people) and computed tomography (CT) scanners (15.4 per million people) just a fraction of the number available in the US (25.9 MRI units per million people and 34.3 CT scanners per million people).[13]

Regulatory System

Germany's Ministry of Health regulates the Health Care industry. It controls the sickness funds, approves reimbursement and medical pricing, sets the framework for health care provisions, determines new drugs and equipment to be included in the benefits package, and establishes the health care budget. Some measures are legislated by government, while others are negotiated between sickness funds and the medical industry. Under the umbrella of the Ministry of Health, there are several agencies that determine the effectiveness of products and services (including cost-benefit analysis), quality control, treatment guidelines, and other measures.

Regarding drug and equipment approval, see the later section discussing the European Medicines Agency (EMA). The EMA not only approves new drugs and equipment, but also whether they may be reimbursed by health insurance plans. As for drugs, manufacturers set their own pricing, and patients are responsible for covering the difference between the drug price and the government reimbursement amount.

FRANCE

France also has a universal health care system. It's the world's fifth largest economy and the fourth largest Health Care market.[14] The World Health Organization (WHO) is a big fan of the nation's system and ranks it the number one health system in the world. That's nice for France and likely something they are proud of, but don't take that to mean French Health Care industries or firms are more profitable than ones elsewhere. Rather, it means they have a lot of what the WHO values, and that's primarily government-funded and -run health care. Whether having universal care results in better care is certainly a hot topic to debate, but when assessing Health Care returns, universal health care hasn't resulted in superior stock returns relative to nations without universal health. And what this book is primarily focused on is how to know if something will drive stock prices.

France's health care system isn't without its own challenges. Budget deficits are a major concern. This limits advancements in capital technology like MRI machines, increases co-pays, and reduces reimbursement coverage and rates. The government is encouraging a more managed-care type of system in which a patient chooses a primary doctor and must get a referral to see specialists. But reduced reimbursements have driven doctors to strike and protest.

Costs and Financing

As of 2009, France spends approximately $300 billion annually on health care—about 11 percent of its GDP.[15] The government funds about 80 percent of the total costs, while the private sector pays roughly 20 percent of the bill.[16]

France's universal health system is funded by an approximately 13.6 percent payroll tax (which the employer pays most of), a 5.25 percent general income tax, and taxes on alcohol, tobacco, and drug manufacturer revenues.[17] Because the system is dependent on tax revenues, budget deficits occur.

France's health care system, though universal, isn't a single-payer system. The government offers basic coverage of physician, hospital, diagnostic testing, prescription drugs, and nursing home costs. Costs are shared with citizens through taxes and by requiring co-pays ranging from 10 percent to 40 percent of expenses—though co-payment requirements decline as individuals get sicker and are less able to work and pay.

Not all costs are covered by the government (more on that in the upcoming section). Coverage and reimbursement rates for hospitals and private practice doctors are negotiated between the insurance funds and unions representing the health care community.

How Residents Get Coverage

French residents get basic coverage primarily through the public, universal insurance program. However, as mentioned earlier, not all costs are covered by the government. Approximately 30 "conditions" (including drugs) are reimbursed 100 percent. As a result, most French residents (over 90 percent) supplement that with private insurance to cover co-payments and other services like some dental and vision expenses.[18] Private insurance premiums may be partially paid by an employer, and similar to Germany, French residents are automatically enrolled based on employment. The retired and unemployed are also covered by insurance. Insurance funds cover 99 percent of residents. The largest single fund, the General Health Insurance Scheme, is for non-agricultural workers and covers about 80 percent of French residents.

Public and private insurance plans are privately managed but heavily regulated—the government sets the premiums, benefits, and reimbursement rates. Insurers cannot compete by lowering prices simply because they don't control the prices—the government does.

How Residents Get Medical Care

Patients are usually free to choose their own doctor and referrals aren't required to see a specialist. Patients pay costs up front and are reimbursed by the government and their private insurance. Because French patients carry medical cards containing microchips that store their medical information and are linked to their bank accounts, reimbursements happen quickly.

Most hospitals are government-managed, non-profit organizations. Just 15 percent of French hospitals are for-profit.[19] For-profit hospitals and clinics mainly focus on minor surgical procedures.

Physicians are generally self-employed and paid on a fee-for-service basis, regardless of whether they work for a government hospital or a private practice. The government sets reimbursement rates, but private practice doctors can charge more if they choose.

The average doctor in France makes about €40,000 (about $57,000 as of 12/31/2009), while the average US doctor makes between $120,000 and $169,000 per year.[20] The lower pay is partially offset by free college tuition and lower malpractice insurance premiums—unlike the US, the French legal system is not nearly as willing to allow medical malpractice lawsuits.[21]

The difference between what the government pays and what a private doctor charges can be covered by co-pays and private insurance, or a patient can pay out of pocket. Hospital doctors, however, have less flexibility to charge above the reimbursement rates.

Regulatory System

The Ministry of Health and Solidarity oversees the health care system, outlines funding needs, and determines what products and services will be approved for reimbursement. It also has several organizations providing advice and guidance.

The French National Authority for Health assesses drugs, equipment, and medical procedures, issues best practices guidelines, certifies doctors, and accredits health care organizations. Its studies and recommendations help the Ministry determine what products and services will be reimbursed—the Ministry generally follows its advice. It is not a government body, but it acts as a liaison between various government health agencies.

The National Authority carries out single technology assessments (STA) and multiple technology assessments (MTA). An STA is required in order for drugs, equipment, or medical procedures to be approved for reimbursement. An STA is the formal process of determining a product or procedure's benefit versus the current standard. A new product will not be covered unless it's better than established products or is less expensive. MTAs review an entire class of products or procedures, and they can also be issued as guidelines.

The French Transparency Commission (*Commission d'Evaluation des Médicaments*) provides scientific advice regarding the quality and benefits of drugs. Its opinion is considered when determining product reimbursement. Product approval is determined by the European Medicines Agency (see upcoming section for more detail).

UNITED KINGDOM

In the UK's universal health care system, the government is the primary payer, with little cost sharing. Contrast this with France, where patients can have meaningful co-payments (which may serve to help keep costs in France down relative to some other universal systems since the consumer is more involved in dictating where money is spent).

The UK is the world's sixth largest economy and fifth largest health care market.[22] The UK encompasses England, Scotland, Northern Ireland, and Wales, with each country responsible for its own budget and expenditures (but residents in one country can obtain medical services in another UK country). UK health care challenges include tight budgets and focus on cost control, which lead to longer waiting times and rationed health care.

Costs and Financing

The UK spends approximately $230 billion annually on health care expenditures, or roughly 8.4 percent of GDP.[23] The government foots about 87 percent of the total bill while the private sector spends roughly 13 percent on out-of-pocket payments and supplemental private insurance.[24] The UK operates largely as a single payer with funding derived through general taxation.

The government establishes a national health care budget, carried out by the National Health Service (NHS). The government tries to adhere to a strict budget on health care expenditures, and it has caused controversy by rejecting treatment for people considered too sick or old. About 10 percent of the public purchases private insurance to provide additional benefits or bypass waiting lists—and the use of private insurance is growing.

Most of the NHS budget is directed to regional trusts (you can think of them like publicly owned companies), which are responsible for negotiating with providers and providing benefits to patients in a local area. There are several types of trusts, but the most commonly known is the Primary Care Trust (PCT). Among other activities, PCTs pay doctors, commission hospitals, develop drug formulary lists, and fund prescriptions. The Primary Care Trusts are grouped into regional Strategic Health Authorities that help develop NHS strategy and enact directives dictated by the Department of Health. Primary Care Trusts have their own budgets and objectives, but Strategic Health Authorities and the Federal Department of Health have overriding power. Trust budgets are supposed to break even and are thus concerned with cost control; however, budget deficits are a major problem.

How Residents Get Coverage

Unlike France and Germany, where coverage is primarily based on work status, the UK offers coverage to all legal residents. Medical care (which includes hospital, doctor, preventative services, mental health, and rehabilitation) is provided free of charge. Dentistry, optometry, and some prescription drugs require a co-pay, but some people, such as children and the elderly, are exempt.

How Residents Get Medical Care

Health care is delivered by general practitioners (GP) based on the location of the patient's residence. GPs provide primary care and act as gatekeepers for access to specialty care doctors. Patients cannot seek specialty services without a referral from their primary doctor.

Most general practitioners, dentists, and optometrists are self-employed and provide services to the NHS under contract. Hospital doctors and nurses are usually employed by the NHS. (The NHS is considered to be one of the largest employers in the world, with over 1 million employees.)[25] Private providers set their own fee-for-service rates and generally are not reimbursed by the public system.

There is a shortage of doctors with only 2.5 practicing physicians per 1,000 people in 2007.[26] This, coupled with government rationing, has led to longer waiting times for patients to see doctors.

Regulatory System

Each country within the UK is responsible for governing its own health care system. In England and Wales, the National Institute for

Health and Clinical Excellence (NICE) sets treatment guidelines and recommends whether a particular treatment should be funded. These guidelines are established by panels of medical experts who specialize in the area being reviewed. Due to budgetary constraints, NICE evaluates drugs and equipment based on cost effectiveness. This generates controversy because some believe the agency denies access to life-saving/extending medicine—the government usually will not pay for NICE-rejected products, which pushes the cost burden onto patients. Additionally, patients must find a doctor willing to administer it since the drug is not listed as a medical guideline.

In Scotland, the Scottish Medicines Consortium advises its NHS about new medicines and formulations of existing medicines. It does not assess vaccines, branded generics, non-prescription-only medicines, blood products and substitutes, or diagnostic drugs. It attempts to render advice within 12 weeks of a newly licensed product.

European Medicines Agency

Each country in the EU determines its own health care budget and reimbursement guidelines. However, the European Medicines Agency (unofficially known as the EMA) is the regulatory body that evaluates and approves new medicine applications, and monitors the safety profiles of existing drugs for all countries within the EU, Iceland, Liechtenstein, and Norway. Based in London, the EMA is considered the European equivalent of the US Food and Drug Administration.

The EMA was set up in 1995 (then known as the European Agency for Evaluation of Medicinal Products) after years of negotiation among EU countries and funded by public and private contributions. The goal was to consolidate various agencies, limit the need for separate country approvals (which is costly), and reduce country favoritism toward local companies. It is a decentralized agency of over 500 employees that incorporate the resources of over 4,500 industry experts.

Structurally, the EMA consists of six scientific committees: The Committee for Medicinal Products for Human Use (CHMP), the Committee for Medicinal Products for Veterinary Use (CVMP), Committee for Orphan Medicinal Products (COMP), Committee on Herbal Medicinal Products (HMPC), the Paediatric Committee (PDCO), and the Committee for Advanced Therapies (CAT). The CHMP is most commonly referred to because this is the committee evaluating adult prescription drugs.

CHINA

China is the world's second largest economy and the sixth largest Health Care market.[27] Still considered an emerging market, China has a health care system unlike any of the developed countries previously discussed in this book. Vast changes over the past 30 years contributed to a chaotic and weak system. Currently, China's health care system is ranked 144 out of 191 nations.[28] Although the ranking methodology is subject to debate, it nevertheless suggests China's health care system has problems, as well as vast opportunities.

China has come a long way in recent decades but still has vast swaths of its population living a basic, subsistence-driven existence. The coastal urban cities have received a lot of attention and have modernized, but inland rural areas have been neglected. The Chinese government is now turning its attention inland, and part of that attention is focused on health care.

Chinese residents typically save a large portion of their income—not because they are inherently thriftier than others, but because, in part, medical expenses are high and most either have no insurance or are vastly underinsured.

The government hopes it can change the country's health care system so citizens can free up some of their savings to spend elsewhere and contribute to China's GDP. China is in the process of building a modern health care system—expanding coverage and improving overall quality. This should also contribute to Chinese citizens becoming healthier overall and spending more on non-health-related items—both strong positives for the economy.

Currently, there are major growth opportunities for Health Care industries in China because the majority of residents continue to use traditional Chinese medicines, including massage, acupuncture, diet management, and herbal remedies. The government also emphasizes preventative medicine because it believes it is more effective than the Western approach to medicine, which generally focuses on curing ailments; despite this, however, Western styles of medicine are becoming more mainstream in the country.

Costs and Funding Mechanism

China spends approximately $200 billion to $250 billion per year on health care expenditures—roughly 5 percent of its GDP.[29] About 60 percent of health expenses are paid out-of-pocket by its citizens and 40 percent is funded by the government.[30] High out-of-pocket expenses are a problem here because the average citizen earns an average of a few hundred dollars per year, while medical expenses can cost tens of thousands of dollars. Similar to other countries, health care expenses have been generally growing faster than GDP.

How Residents Get Coverage and Care

Prior to 1978, the government provided all health care services. The government paid for all medical equipment, hospitals, staff salaries (including doctors), and operating expenses.

In 1978, the government moved toward reducing direct involvement and privatizing the system, which consisted of three tiers based on the level of care required. In cities, medical personnel worked in local neighborhoods to treat minor concerns. If patients needed more care, they were sent to district hospitals. Patients with the most serious medical conditions were sent to municipal hospitals.

The rural areas of China had a similar system to the urban areas. The first tier consisted of "barefoot doctors," who were primarily farmers with minimal medical training. They treated common illnesses and promoted basic hygiene and preventative health care.

Barefoot doctors got the name because some farmed rice paddies barefoot. The second and third tiers are similar in nature to the urban system.

The tiered system quickly folded after the government began privatizing businesses and ceased funding support. This change led to a dramatic decrease in health care coverage as barefoot doctors left to make more money in areas like farming or entered private practice where they worked on a fee-for-service basis. Out-of-pocket costs became quite expensive, and hospitals required upfront payments, forcing Chinese citizens to save a high portion of their income. Even those with insurance coverage were faced with large out-of-pocket expenses (reimbursements were as low as 20 percent) and high premiums.[31]

Vast health care disparities, high out-of-pocket costs, and many uninsured citizens resulted from the government's policy change. The system was failing, and in 1997, the government established the Basic Health Insurance Scheme (BHIS) for urban residents. Similar to the systems in Germany and France, it is an employment-based system in which employees and employers make contributions to a common fund. All companies are required to join BHIS to provide insurance for their employees.

BHIS requires co-pays, and patients use specific facilities to cut costs. Only drugs and services approved by the BHIS are eligible for reimbursement. It also provides limited coverage (for example, it does not cover dependants). Enforcement has been weak, however, and some employers choose not to join BHIS to save money. Commercial health insurance plans, an alternative option, are limited to certain cities, and premiums are high. As a consequence of high costs and limited coverage, China's 2003 Third National Public Health Survey showed about 45 percent of China's urban residents and 79 percent of rural residents did not have any insurance coverage.[32]

Since costs have remained high and many citizens uninsured, in 2006, Chinese President Hu Jintao stated all citizens should have access to care. After years of negotiations, the government announced in 2009 a goal to provide universal health care to all citizens by 2020. It committed to spend $124 billion to improve and build hospitals

and clinics, expand insurance coverage to all citizens, reduce disparities between regions, and improve overall quality.

Regulatory System

China's Ministry of Health oversees the health care system. It is
responsible for providing information, raising health care awareness,
providing access to health care, monitoring and coordinating health
quality and utilization, and acting as liaison between China and other
organizations outside the country.

But regulations are underdeveloped and poorly enforced, and monitoring capacity is weak. Most health facilities lack a formal governance system, and quality of care irregularities are prevalent. Inappropriate financial
incentives, lack of clinical treatment guidelines, inadequate government
resource allocation, weak regulation among service providers, and low
capacity of health care personnel have resulted in poor quality of care.[33]

Safety standards and regulations pertaining to food, medicines,
blood, hospitals, and laboratories are inconsistent. Weaknesses in
safety regulation and enforcement are particularly apparent in rural
areas, where township and village businesses operate in a largely
unregulated fashion and generate the majority of occupational diseases, disabilities, and deaths.

China is highly sensitive to drug pricing since drugs account for
approximately 44 percent of total health expenditures, compared to
about 10 percent in the US.[34] The BHIS formulary is maintained by
the Ministry of Labor and Social Security. (A formulary is a list of drugs
and services the payer will fund, and it's important for companies to get
their products and services on the list—this concept is discussed in later
chapters.) The formulary's goal is to provide basic drug coverage and
contain costs. Therefore, the BHIS provides limited coverage.

The National Development and Reform Commission is responsible for setting ceiling retail prices for BHIS formulary drugs and other
drugs not on the list. Ceiling prices allow companies to earn a profit
margin above their costs. Higher margins are given to new drugs, higher
quality drugs, and drugs under patents to encourage innovations.

Chapter Recap

Understanding the Health Care sector wouldn't be complete without a basic knowledge of how some of the largest health care systems operate around the world. Combined with the US market, the countries discussed in this chapter make up nearly two-thirds of the global Health Care market. Understanding how a country's health care system operates will help you gain insight on how Health Care firms are regulated and do business in each respective country. Key points to remember:

- The developed countries discussed offer some type of government-funded universal health care coverage.
  - Coverage is provided through employers or directly by the government.
  - Patient co-pays vary across countries.
  - Some countries have a gatekeeper system while others do not.
  - Use of private insurance is limited.
  - Wait times vary across countries.
  - Cost control is vital and budgets have been pressured.
  - Understanding the political and regulatory system is vital to doing business in each country.
- China is an emerging country with high uninsured rates and out-of-pocket expenses.
  - The country has witnessed many changes to its health care system, making it chaotic.
  - The government is trying to move toward a universal system by 2020.
  - The regulatory system is relatively weak.

4

HEALTH CARE SECTOR DRIVERS

To start, what exactly is a "driver"? Drivers can be anything that influences—positively or negatively—a firm's revenue, earnings, and/or stock price. However, our focus as investors and the focus of this chapter will be stock price drivers—determining a sector's, industry's, or firm's chief drivers and evaluating how they affect stock prices over the next 12 to 18 months are imperative to making better investments.

This chapter outlines some of the important macro drivers for the Health Care sector. In particular, this chapter discusses the main drivers that position the Health Care sector, on a macro level, to outperform the broader market. There are three main categories of drivers you can use to examine the forward-looking prospects of the sector. These include:

1. The defensive nature of Health Care
2. Innovation/patent expirations
3. Political/regulatory developments

While the industries within the Health Care sector are not as wildly varied as some other sectors, like Industrials, they're not homogeneous, either. This means that what drives earnings and stock prices in the drug industry may not necessarily impact health insurers' earnings and stock prices, for example. However, there are prevailing macro factors that can impact the overall sector's relative performance—which is the subject of this chapter. Industry-specific drivers are covered in Chapter 5.

DEFENSIVE NATURE OF HEALTH CARE

Historically, the Health Care sector has typically been less economically sensitive—also described as "defensive"—meaning it tends to do relatively better than the broader market when the economy isn't growing particularly fast or is in a recession. This doesn't mean Health Care tends to have negative returns during periods of strong growth. It may post positive returns, just typically not as strong as more economically sensitive sectors, like Consumer Discretionary or Materials—which may also be described as "cyclical."

Why is Health Care more defensive? Most Health Care goods and services have fairly inelastic demand (see the nearby box)—meaning demand doesn't fall as much during economic downturns. Investors therefore anticipate the Health Care sector is likely to hold up better during a recession and may look to it as a relative safe haven—which can help it outperform the broad market during those periods.

Though Health Care is traditionally considered defensive, that doesn't mean it will always behave that way—either at a sector level or within its individual industries. There are, however, reasons why Health Care has occasionally done relatively well (and may do well in the future) during periods of strong growth. Health Care analysis cannot simply be an analysis of whether there will be economic slowdown or not. Like all sectors, there are myriad drivers that interplay—it's important to understand what might make Health Care perform like a traditionally defensive sector and what might make it behave more cyclically.

Elastic Versus Inelastic

We frequently refer to demand as being *elastic* or *inelastic*. But what does it mean? Pretty much what it sounds like—elastic demand can stretch or snap back, while there's not much bounce to inelastic demand.

An easy way to understand this is to think about what makes people buy certain things. If the economy is cooking along, folks are more likely to be earning a good and growing wage. They feel confident about the future and are likely to splurge on a new TV or home electronics or a vacation. What they don't do is buy twice as much toothpaste or heart medication just because times are flush.

Conversely, when the economy slows, folks may feel less confident. They might hunker down and delay upgrading their computer or taking a fancy trip. However, their teeth still need brushing and their hearts still need the medication; demand for items considered essential doesn't expand much nor snap back much—it's inelastic. And that's the case with Health Care—most of the goods and services from this sector are considered, for the most part, essential. Investors expect demand to stay fairly steady, so they tend to prefer these types of stocks if they anticipate a downturn.

Economic Strength

Since Health Care is defensive in nature, it generally makes sense to increase your exposure to the sector when you expect the economy to be weak or contracting. The best way to measure economic growth (and hence help your weighting decision) is a country's GDP—whether in the US or globally. But GDP is released quarterly at a month lag, then revised twice (in the US and most places)—so while useful, it is inherently backward-looking and tells nothing about where the economy is heading. But considered against a backdrop of other indicators, it can help you paint a fuller picture of the current environment and help you shape your forward-looking expectations. Economic forecasting is itself a rigorous discipline outside the scope of this book. However, if you believe an economic slowdown is the most likely outcome in the next 12 to 18 months, history shows that is typically a good time to overweight Health Care stocks.

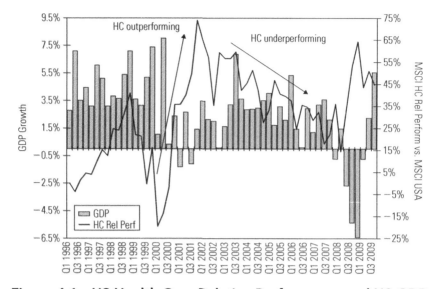

Figure 4.1   US Health Care Relative Performance and US GDP

Source: Thomson Reuters, MSCI Inc.[1] MSCI USA Price Index, MSCI USA Health Care Price Index, from 1996–2009.

Relative Performance and GDP   Figure 4.1 illustrates the defensive nature of Health Care at work. The line represents the relative performance of Health Care—when the line is going up, Health Care is outperforming the broad market. When it is falling, it is underperforming. The bars represent GDP growth per quarter. Generally, during this period, Health Care outperformed when GDP was weak or declining. But not always! You can see Health Care also outperformed through most of the mid to late 1990s, a period of vibrant GDP growth.

Interest Rates and Access to Credit

Because Health Care is defensive in nature, it also typically does better than the market when credit conditions are less than ideal. (A good way to know whether credit conditions are looser or tighter is by watching interest rates.)

Broadly, there are two types of interest rates. Central bank rates (like the US Federal Funds Target Rate) are controlled either directly or indirectly by a nation's central bank. All other interest rates are set by the market. They can and do move independently of central bank rates and represent an entity's cost of borrowing.

Benign interest rates generally translate into lower borrowing costs, and higher interest rates make borrowing more expensive. Thus, firms that rely more on debt financing face more headwinds from higher interest rates compared to less debt-intensive firms. Health Care firms traditionally have less debt on their balance sheets, generate relatively stable cash flows, and are not very debt dependent to support operations. This contributes to the sector's defensive nature.

This was highlighted during the credit crisis of 2008 and 2009. Debt-heavy companies were severely punished by the market, while many of the largest Health Care firms retained easy access to credit during the crisis due to their relatively lower levels of leverage—low debt levels and easy access to credit helped the Health Care sector outperform the overall market.

INNOVATION AND PATENT EXPIRATIONS

Health Care is typically defensive, but that doesn't mean it can't be a strong performer even during a healthy economic expansion. So what can make this classically defensive sector outperform during an economic expansion? Or even achieve particularly strong outperformance during a period of weaker growth? Innovation! A major reason Health Care performed so well in the mid to late 1990s (see Figure 4.1) was that Health Care firms launched a variety of new and in-demand products during this period. Innovation is the hallmark of a healthy Health Care industry. Companies can outperform the sector or even the broader market when they are launching new and unique products. Conversely, the market becomes concerned and shares underperform when patents expire and companies aren't launching new products to sustain growth.

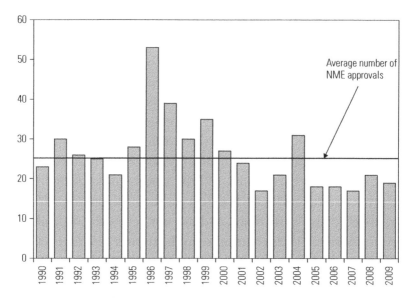

Figure 4.2   Number of NME Approvals by the FDA
Source: FDA; data does not include all biologics; from 1990 to 2009.

Figure 4.2 illustrates the number of new molecular entities (NMEs) approved by the FDA over the last 20 years. NMEs are typically new and innovative drugs. (See Chapter 5 for more on NMEs.) As Figure 4.2 shows, the number of new drugs approved during the mid to late 1990s was consistently above average, contributing to sector outperformance during that time. The fewer number of drugs approved during much of the 2000s, particularly later in the decade, contributed to the Pharmaceutical industry's (and overall sector's) performance lag.

Partially influencing the reduced number of approvals during the late 2000s was a stricter regulatory environment as a result of Merck's troubles with its painkiller drug Vioxx in 2004 (see Chapter 6 for more on Vioxx). In light of the Vioxx debacle, legislators partially blamed the FDA for not adequately supervising the safety profile of drugs. The FDA has taken steps to increase oversight, and, coincidentally (or not), the number of drugs approved after 2004 was below average.

Helping to explain the below-average number of NME approvals during the late 2000s (and relative sector underperformance) was not only a stricter FDA, but a general lack of innovative products. Companies that benefited from the 1990s innovation boom were starting to see those patents expire and didn't innovate enough new products to offset the upcoming patent losses. Thus, the industry was dealing with two problems at the same time—a lack of innovative products and push back on the pipeline products they did have from a stricter FDA.

It's one thing to see how many drugs have been approved, but how can you determine whether a company has innovative new products on the horizon? Look at the pipeline! As you will see in subsequent chapters, Health Care companies disclose their pipelines and will even project expected launch dates as products get close to regulatory review. Patent expiration dates are known in advance as well. Pipelines and expected launch dates are by no means a guarantee of future success, but they can certainly help you determine whether a firm has favorable prospects or not. Pipelines are a probabilities game, and whoever has the largest pipeline tends to have a greater chance of success.

POLITICAL/REGULATORY DEVELOPMENTS

What happens in Washington can influence what happens on Wall Street—always been that way, probably always will. So it's worthwhile to understand the most significant political drivers most relevant to the Health Care sector, including:

- Government expenditures
- Legislation and regulation
- Taxes

Government Expenditures

Governments are the largest payers of health care globally. Their size often allows them to dictate how much they will pay for products and services. Generally, the government doesn't make broad sweeping changes to spending, such as increasing spending for all health care products. Therefore, it is important to understand which industries the government is increasing and decreasing payments to. It is also important to follow government plans to increase or decrease research funding because this has a residual impact on health care demand. And sudden, unexpected changes can have a big impact on stock price direction.

Legislation and Regulation

Health Care is heavily regulated, and politicians frequently attempt to alter the playing field. It is extremely important to understand changes and developments taking place because they can have material ramifications on the sector.

One example of legislation impacting Health Care performance was the 1993 to 1994 health care debate in which President Bill Clinton proposed universal health care for all Americans. "Hillary Care," as it became known because First Lady Hillary Clinton championed the cause, generated a vast amount of uncertainty within the industry and caused the sector to lag. Conversely, the sector began to outperform in the mid to late 1990s when the market began to anticipate Hillary Care would fail, which it eventually did. Figure 4.1 shows Health Care outperforming the broader market in the late 1990s, partially due to innovation and partially due to legislative recovery.

Uncertainty also occurred during the 2009 health care debate to reform the system in the United States. Topics debated and considered were universal health care; the government crowding out private insurers by creating its own insurance company; taxing health insurance companies; levying fees on pharmaceuticals, equipment, and health insurance firms; and negotiating lower revenue concessions with the Pharmaceutical and Health Care Provider & Services industries. Even though the reform was passed in 2010, investors still don't know how the new laws will be interpreted and implemented. All these topics created vast uncertainty since they could alter the business landscape.

Aside from politics, regulatory bodies like the FDA can have a tremendous impact (positive or negative) on a firm because they are responsible for reviewing and approving or rejecting new product applications. Some products are not allowed to be sold commercially unless approved. Regulatory bodies are constantly reviewing the safety profile of currently marketed products, and they can require companies to increase warning labels on them, which can materially impact sales, denting investor sentiment on the stocks.

Taxes

Tax policy is capable of materially impacting any company, sector, or overall market. Increased industry taxes and fees could stifle innovation, sales and earnings, and ultimately share price performance. For example, the 2010 US health care legislation imposes new taxes and fees on pharmaceutical, equipment, health insurance, and other companies. New taxes and fees could adversely impact industry players, depending on whether the companies can offset these new costs with higher revenues and efficiency gains.

Many Health Care firms have both domestic and foreign operations. These international operations are subject to the local tax code of the country where they're located. But, for example, parent companies located in the US face repatriation taxes—funds brought back into the US from a foreign subsidiary are often subject to additional taxes. As such, it's likely the sector would react negatively if the US government forced corporations to repatriate funds or significantly raised repatriation tax rates. This would be a bearish driver.

Chapter Recap

The Health Care sector has a multitude of drivers that dictate the sector's relative performance. The major drivers are:

- Defensive nature of Health Care: The Health Care sector frequently outperforms during times of economic and market weakness.
- Innovation: The sector tends to perform well when launching new and innovative products.
- Political/regulatory developments: Uncertainty surrounding regulatory or legislative reform can weigh on sector performance.

II

NEXT STEPS: HEALTH CARE DETAILS

5

HEALTH CARE SECTOR BREAKDOWN

Now that you have a high-level understanding of the Health Care sector and its origins, it's time to explore the industries making up the sector. We'll cover each industry by asking four fundamental questions:

1. How big is the market?
2. Who are the biggest players?
3. How does the industry operate?
4. What are the industry drivers?

Answering these questions provides insight into the basic framework of each Health Care industry. Armed with this knowledge, you can better understand the variables business managers in the sector deal with day to day, which can make you a better investor.

This chapter can serve as a reference guide to use when seeking a refresher on industries you may consider investing in. With that in mind, feel free to skip around if you're particularly interested in certain industries.

GLOBAL INDUSTRY CLASSIFICATION STANDARD

Before beginning, some definitions: The Global Industry Classification Standard (GICS) is a widely accepted framework for classifying companies into groups based on similarities. The GICS structure consists of 10 sectors, 24 industry groups, 68 industries, and 154 sub-industries. This structure offers four levels of hierarchy, ranging from the most general sector to the most specialized sub-industry:

- Sector
- Industry group
- Industry
- Sub-industry

Let's start by breaking down the Health Care sector into its different components. According to GICS, the Health Care sector consists of 2 industry groups, 6 industries, and 10 sub-industries.

Industry Group: Pharmaceuticals, Biotechnology & Life Sciences

1. Industry: Pharmaceuticals
    i. Sub-Industry: Pharmaceuticals
2. Industry: Biotechnology
    ii. Sub-Industry: Biotechnology
3. Industry: Life Sciences Tools & Services
    iii. Sub-Industry: Life Sciences Tools & Services

Industry Group: Health Care Equipment & Services

4. Industry: Health Care Equipment & Supplies
    iv. Sub-Industry: Health Care Equipment
    v. Sub-Industry: Health Care Supplies
5. Industry: Health Care Providers & Services
    vi. Sub-Industry: Health Care Distributors
    vii. Sub-Industry: Health Care Facilities
    viii. Sub-Industry: Health Care Services
    ix. Sub-Industry: Managed Health Care

6. Industry: Health Care Technology

    x. Sub-Industry: Health Care Technology

But before delving deeper into the industries and sub-industries, it's vital to understand what Health Care looks like globally and how it fits into a broader benchmark.

GLOBAL HEALTH CARE BENCHMARKS

What's a benchmark? What does it do, and why is it necessary? A benchmark is your guide for building a stock portfolio. You can use any well-constructed index as a benchmark—examples are in Table 5.1. By studying a benchmark's (i.e., the index's) makeup, investors can assign expected risk and return to make underweight and overweight decisions for each industry. This is just as true for a sector as it is for the broader stock market, and there are many potential Health Care sector benchmarks to choose from. (Benchmarks will be further explored with the top-down method in Chapter 7.)

Differences in Benchmarks

So what does the Health Care investment universe look like? It depends on the benchmark, so choose carefully! The large-cap US Health Care sector looks different from small cap, and emerging markets (EM) looks different from the developed world. Table 5.1 shows major domestic and international benchmark indexes and the percentage weight of each sector.

Sector weights show each sector's relative importance in driving overall index performance. While Health Care is one of the larger weights in the Russell 2000, it's one of the smallest in the MSCI EM. Why the large-cap and developed-world bias? Much of the difference can be attributed to the vast market share and international footprint many of the world's largest firms possess. Emerging markets generally don't have the financial resources or infrastructure the developed world does. Developed-world firms are big sellers to emerging

Table 5.1   Benchmark Differences

Sector	MSCI ACWI (All-Country World Index)	MSCI World (Developed World)	MSCI EAFE (Developed World ex-US)	S&P 500 (Large Cap US)	Russell 2000 (Small Cap US)	MSCI Emerging Markets (Emerging Markets)
Consumer Discretionary	8.9%	9.3%	9.7%	9.5%	13.8%	5.7%
Consumer Staples	9.6%	10.2%	10.1%	11.4%	3.5%	5.7%
Energy	11.4%	10.9%	8.4%	11.5%	5.2%	14.7%
Financials	21.1%	20.6%	24.5%	14.4%	20.3%	24.3%
Health Care	**9.0%**	**10.1%**	**8.4%**	**12.6%**	**14.3%**	**2.2%**
Industrials	9.9%	10.4%	11.2%	10.2%	15.7%	6.7%
Information Technology	12.2%	12.0%	4.8%	19.9%	18.3%	13.5%
Materials	8.5%	7.5%	10.4%	3.6%	4.8%	14.9%
Telecommuni-cation Services	4.9%	4.4%	5.8%	3.2%	1.0%	8.6%
Utilities	4.5%	4.6%	5.9%	3.7%	3.2%	3.7%
Total	**100%**	**100%**	**100%**	**100%**	**100%**	100%

Source: Thomson Reuters, MSCI, Inc.[1] as of 12/31/2009.

markets, which helps explain the relatively small Health Care weight in EM. Successful small-cap firms, meanwhile, are likely to be bought by the big guys, so there's some survivorship bias.

Table 5.1 shows the Health Care sector comprises about 9 percent of the developed-world market (based on the MSCI World benchmark). Utilizing a global top-down investment strategy and assuming the MSCI World Index is your selected benchmark, you can use this percentage as a rough gauge for how much you should allocate to Health Care stocks in your portfolio. (Note: How to formulate more precise allocations based on your perception of market conditions will be discussed in later chapters.)

Sector weight deviations can also occur from country to country, as shown in Table 5.2, which includes selected countries from the MSCI All Country World Index (MSCI ACWI). The US is

Table 5.2   Health Care Weights by Country

Country	% of MSCI ACWI Health Care
US	59.8%
Switzerland	11.1%
UK	8.3%
Japan	5.5%
France	4.0%
Germany	3.8%
Israel	2.5%
Denmark	1.9%
Australia	1.2%
India	0.4%
South Africa	0.2%
Sweden	0.2%
Belgium	0.2%
Ireland	0.2%
Hungary	0.1%
Canada	0.1%
Korea	0.1%
Russia	0.1%
China	0.1%
Finland	0.1%
Spain	0.1%

Source: Thomson Reuters; MSCI, Inc.[2] as of 12/31/2009.

nearly five times the next largest country weight. Table 5.2 should look familiar (it was presented in Chapter 1). Knowing the country weights within Health Care will help guide your allocation decisions.

Knowing the benchmark sector weight is a helpful starting point, but there's a critical question left to answer—what kind of Health Care stocks do you want to own? You can refine your search by looking at the industry breakdown of the sector, which we've demonstrated for some of the key benchmarks in Table 5.3. Once you've decided to allocate a certain percentage of your portfolio toward the Health Care sector, Table 5.3 can provide a starting point for allocating within the sector.

Table 5.3   Health Care Sub-Industry Weights

Sub-Industry	MSCI ACWI (All Country World Index)	MSCI World (Developed World)	MSCI EAFE (Developed World ex-US)	S&P 500 (Large Cap US)	Russell 2000 (Small Cap US)	MSCI Emerging Markets (Emerging Markets)
Pharmaceuticals	62.3%	61.1%	83.3%	49.6%	10.6%	95.6%
Health Care Equipment	13.4%	13.9%	7.9%	15.3%	18.0%	0.0%
Biotechnology	8.6%	8.9%	2.8%	12.3%	27.6%	0.0%
Health Care Services	4.4%	4.6%	1.9%	6.5%	12.0%	0.0%
Managed Health Care	4.2%	4.4%	0.0%	7.7%	5.5%	0.0%
Life Sciences Tools & Services	3.1%	3.2%	1.1%	3.8%	5.1%	0.0%
Health Care Distributors	2.7%	2.7%	1.2%	3.6%	3.1%	0.0%
Health Care Supplies	1.0%	1.0%	1.9%	0.4%	7.2%	2.2%
Health Care Technology	0.3%	0.3%	0.0%	0.5%	5.3%	0.0%
Health Care Facilities	0.1%	0.0%	0.0%	0.2%	5.6%	2.2%

Source: Thomson Reuters, MSCI, Inc.[3] as of 12/31/2009.

PHARMACEUTICALS, BIOTECHNOLOGY & LIFE SCIENCES

Here we'll look at the industries and sub-industries themselves. As we examine each industry (or sub-industry), we'll focus primarily on four factors:

1. Market size
2. Biggest players
3. Modes of operation
4. Unique industry drivers

As a reminder, GICS breaks down the Pharmaceuticals, Biotechnology & Life Sciences industry group into three industries and sub-industries:

1. Pharmaceuticals
    i. Pharmaceuticals
2. Biotechnology
    ii. Biotechnology
3. Life Sciences Tools & Services
    iii. Life Sciences Tools & Services

This industry group's industries and sub-industries share the same name because they are fairly narrow and focused. You will see later other industries are broken down into various sub-industries with different titles. Again, the industry and sub-industry classification is derived by GICS. Because this group represents approximately 75 percent of the entire sector, understanding how this group operates is vital to analyzing the overall sector.

The Pharmaceuticals industry includes firms that discover, develop, manufacture, and sell prescription (also known as *ethical*) drugs to treat humans and animals. The Biotechnology industry is similar to the Pharmaceuticals industry because the Biotech industry also discovers, manufactures, and sells prescription drugs. Biotech's and Pharmaceutical's drivers are similar as well.

Still, there are some major differences between Pharma and Biotech. The first is the composition of the drugs themselves. In general, Pharmaceuticals' drugs are composed of chemicals and are called "small molecules." Biotech drugs are composed of living organisms like proteins and are called "large molecules." Small molecule drugs are absorbed through the body while large molecules often cannot pass through cell membranes, so it's common for biotech drugs to be injected directly into the bloodstream. Biotech drugs also tend to target specific diseases with no currently known cures, such as HIV/AIDS. As a result, Biotech drugs can command premium pricing—some drugs can cost over $200,000 dollars per year. Consequently, one or two drugs may drive nearly all of a Biotech firm's revenues while traditional Pharma companies tend to be more diversified.

Because many Biotech and Pharmaceutical firms now work together to produce and distribute drugs, the two are becoming increasingly interconnected (e.g., a Pharma firm might own a Biotech company).

Sometimes, the two industries are referred to as the *bio-pharmaceutical* industry, or bio-pharma. Although GICS currently separates the two industries, it wouldn't be surprising to see them combined one day.

The Life Sciences industry generally supports the bio-pharma industry by providing analytical tools, equipment, and supplies. Life Sciences companies can also provide clinical trial and other research services.

The Drug Industry

Since the Pharmaceuticals and Biotech industries are similar with similar drivers, we'll refer to them both as the drug industry for this section. In aggregate, Pharmaceuticals' market capitalization is over $1.5 trillion while the Biotechnology industry is nearly $200 billion. Combined, the drug industry represents roughly 74 percent of the MSCI ACWI Health Care benchmark. Tables 5.4 and 5.5 provide the 10 largest Pharmaceutical and Biotech companies around the world, listed by market capitalization.

GICS doesn't break down Pharmaceuticals any further, but there are different types of firms in this industry: *pharmaceuticals, generics, and diversified pharmaceuticals.* Pharmaceuticals are "pure play" firms

Table 5.4   Ten Largest Branded Pharmaceuticals Companies

Rank	Company	Market Cap ($Mil)	Country
1	Johnson & Johnson	$164,853	US
2	Novartis	$131,065	Switzerland
3	Roche	$111,768	Switzerland
4	Pfizer	$110,686	US
5	GlaxoSmithKline	$100,850	UK
6	Sanofi-Aventis	$95,843	France
7	Abbot Laboratories	$77,806	US
8	Merck & Co.	$66,999	US
9	AstraZeneca	$64,416	UK
10	Bayer	$64,306	Germany

Note: All companies may not be listed in the MSCI ACWI Managed Health Care Index.
Source: Bloomberg Finance, L.P., Thomson Reuters, MSCI, Inc.,[4] as of 12/31/2009.

Table 5.5   Ten Largest Biotechnology Companies

Rank	Company	Market Cap ($Mil)	Country
1	Amgen	$56,287	US
2	Gilead Sciences	$40,891	US
3	Celgene	$25,013	US
4	CSL	$17,673	Australia
5	Genzyme	$15,086	US
6	Biogen Idec	$14,038	US
7	Actelion	$7,809	Switzerland
8	Vertex Pharms	$5,991	US
9	Cephalon	$4,008	US
10	Griflols	$3,948	Spain

Note: All companies may not be listed in the MSCI ACWI Managed Health Care Index.
Source: Bloomberg Finance, L.P., Thomson Reuters, MSCI, Inc.,[5] as of 12/31/2009.

that develop and sell innovative "branded" drugs. (Pure play companies are firms that concentrate only on one business.) Generic pharmaceutical firms sell just that, generic versions of branded drugs. Diversified pharmaceuticals can sell a myriad of products, such as branded and generic drugs, health care equipment, consumer products, and diagnostic tests. When talking about drugs, another important distinction to make is between branded and generics.

Branded Drugs

The branded drug business operates in a high risk/high reward environment. Some estimate only 1 of every 5,000 to 10,000 potential drug candidates will make it to market.[6] Further, only about 20 percent of marketed drugs are profitable. Firms also launch drugs similar to others already on the market—these "me too" drugs generally cannot command premium pricing due to competition and pricing pressures from insurance firms and government. However, the few unique and successful drugs can achieve pricing power and substantial profits, more than offsetting the failed products. Drug firms can have among the highest profit margins of any industry—but there are fewer than 100 drugs generating more than $1 billion in sales

Table 5.6   World's Top-Selling Drugs—2009

Company	Drug Name	Treatment	Sales ($Bil)
Pfizer/Astellas	Lipitor	Cholesterol	$13.20
Bristol-Myers/Sanofi-Aventis	Plavix	Anti-blood clot	$9.10
AstraZeneca	Nexium	Heartburn	$8.20
GlaxoSmithKline	Advair/Seretide	Asthma	$8.10
AstraZeneca	Seroquel	Depression, bipolar disorder, schizophrenia	$6.00
Amgen	Enbrel	Arthritis, psoriasis	$5.90
Johnson & Johnson	Remicade	Arthritis, psoriasis	$5.50
AstraZeneca	Crestor	Cholesterol	$5.40
Eli Lilly	Zyprexa	Bipolar disorder, schizophrenia	$5.40
Abbott Labs	Humira	Arthritis, psoriasis	$5.00
Roche	Avastin	Colon, lung, breast, kidney cancer	$5.00
Merck	Singulair	Asthma/allergy	$4.90
Roche	MabThera/Rituxin	Non-Hodgkin's lymphoma, leukemia	$4.70
Bristol-Myers Squibb	Abilify	Depression, bipolar disorder, schizophrenia	$4.70
Sanofi-Aventis	Lovenox	Deep vein thrombosis	$4.60

Source: IMS Health, "Top 15 Global Products, 2009, Total Audited Markets."

(known as blockbuster drugs).[7] Table 5.6 lists the top 15 drugs by revenues.

Drug Patents and Lifecycle   Research and development (R&D) is the lifeblood of the drug industry. Drug firms must launch new drugs on a regular basis because each drug's revenue and profit, particularly for pharmaceuticals, is limited by the length of time remaining on its patent. In most of the developed world, a drug's patent lasts 20 years, giving the drug company exclusive rights to the product. Upon patent expiration, other firms are allowed to sell the product—hence, generic versions become available, and a branded product may lose 80 percent or more of its revenues. As a result, drug firms may try to extend patents via new manufacturing methods, different inactive ingredients, receiving approval for treating other diseases, or paying generic companies to delay launching generic versions.

Twenty-year patent protection may seem like a long time—but the patent is initiated at the onset of drug discovery, and it takes an average of 10 years to bring a drug to market. This typically gives a company about 10 years to sell the drug, recoup its investment, and turn a profit. It usually takes several years for a drug to reach peak sales because doctor and patient acceptance takes time.

Biotech is unique in that the US does not currently allow biogenerics, also known as biosimilars or bioequivalents. Biogenerics are prohibited because it's more difficult to develop and manufacture biotech drugs. Since biotech drugs are made from living organisms, which are unique, some argue a generic firm without the exact cell line would not be able to manufacture the same drug. Because the bioequivalent wouldn't be exactly the same, it's suggested biogenerics also go through clinical trials. The European Union (EU) approved biogenerics in 2006, and the few on the market sell at a discount of about 20 percent to 30 percent. Additionally, in 2010, US legislation granted the FDA authority to approve generic biologics. The fact that biotech drugs have not encountered generic competition to the extent pharmaceuticals have makes it very compelling for the Pharmaceuticals industry to enter the biotech business.

Major Types of Drug Patents

- Composition of matter (the drug itself)
- Process (the way it's made)
- Use (ailment the drug is used to treat)
- Delivery method

A drug's patent can be extended six months beyond the original patent expiration if a company submits pediatric drug trial data. This "pediatric extension" encourages companies to test for drug safety and efficacy in children, which generally has not been standard practice.

Drug Development Process   A new drug, also known as a new molecular entity (NME), must go through rigorous testing before it can be approved to be marketed. The testing phase can take years and can cost $1 billion or more. The drug business has enormous barriers to entry tied to high costs and regulatory requirements to bring drugs to market. The drug industry spends over $100 billion per year on R&D, averaging about 15 percent to 20 percent of a firm's sales. However, R&D as a percentage of sales across individual companies can range from 10 percent to 40 percent or more.

Regulatory groups, like the Food and Drug Administration (FDA) and the European Medicines Agency (EMA), require a drug to pass three clinical phases of human testing before it can be approved. However, before human trials can even begin, preclinical studies are conducted in test tubes and animals for efficacy and toxicity. If preclinical trials warrant further investigation, the company submits an Investigational New Drug (IND) application to begin human trials.

During Phase I, a small group of about 30 healthy volunteers will be used to determine a drug's safety profile (although sometimes real patients are used). The trials are often conducted in hospitals where a full-time staff can monitor the test subjects.

A larger group of patients (up to a few hundred) is involved in Phase II trials to continue studying safety, dosing, tolerability, and also to see if the drug actually works. Placebos (fake, inactive drugs) may be used during this phase to determine how well the drug works against a control population.

Drugs passing Phase II enter Phase III, the longest (it can last several years) and most expensive part of the process. A large group of patients (up to several thousand) participate in testing to determine safety, efficacy, and proper dosing. Most tests involve placebos where neither the administering doctor nor the patient knows who's getting the actual and fake drug. This process, called double-blind testing, attempts to reduce bias in the test. Many times, the trial drug is compared to a similar drug already approved to see how the drug performs.

Did You Know?

Companies continue to conduct research on marketed products because it can be difficult to find every potential safety problem during clinical development. This continued research is sometimes referred to as Phase IV testing.

Comparing drugs during the testing phase can help determine eventual pricing. If the drug is deemed to far outperform what's already on the market, then the drug company can achieve pricing power. Conversely, there is less pricing power if it is a "me too" product.

When a company believes its drug is ready to be approved for marketing in the US, pharmaceutical drugs are presented to the FDA in the form of a New Drug Application (NDA), biologics are submitted to the FDA in the form of a Biologic License Application (BLA), and animal drugs are submitted to the FDA in the form of a New Animal Drug Application (NADA). Companies submitting drug applications pay a fee as part of the Prescription Drug User Fee Act (PDUFA)—the fee helps the FDA hire and retain personnel to review the applications, which can be over 50,000 pages. User fees are roughly 25 percent of the FDA's annual budget.

The FDA may take a few to several months to act on the application, depending on whether the drug is listed as a priority review. It may approve the application or request additional data and information before approval. Requesting additional information, known as "approval letters," can delay drug approval months to years and may cause companies to drop a product altogether. On average, it takes the FDA 18 months to review an application and render a decision (though it can also take as little as 6 months or as long as several years).

Orphan drugs target rare diseases, and the Orphan Drug Act provides subsidies and exclusive market rights to incentivize companies to develop drugs they otherwise wouldn't consider.

Marketing   Companies begin selling their products upon regulatory (e.g., FDA, EMA) approval. Marketing expenses are often the largest expense a drug company incurs, even larger than its massive R&D budget. Selling, general, and administrative (SG&A) expenses as a percentage of sales can average around the 25 to 40 percent range, meaning SG&A expenses double R&D efforts.

Drug firms typically employ sales reps to market products directly to doctors, and some of the largest firms employ thousands of reps to visit doctors on a regular basis. But some firms don't have the capacity to manufacture or distribute their products, so they may license their products to another firm with the capabilities.

However, marketing efforts are shifting toward insurance companies and governments—those who pay the bills. The payers have a list of approved drugs they will pay for, called a formulary list. Therefore, it's critical for a firm to get its drug on the list.

A formulary list generally has three to five "tiers." The patient pays a greater co-pay for higher tier levels and lower for lower tier levels. For example, tier one drugs may be generic drugs with a $10 co-pay. Tier two drugs may be preferred branded drugs with co-pays ranging from $20 to $50. Tier three drugs may be nonpreferred branded drugs with co-pays ranging from $50 to $100. Typically, a lower cost for branded drugs should increase demand, so firms generally prefer to have their drugs on the tier two formulary list.

Drug firms increasingly use direct-to-consumer (DTC) advertising in an attempt to get patients to demand, or at least inquire about, their products. As long as the drug is effective and safe, doctors generally don't mind prescribing medicine a patient demands. In the US, marketing and distribution is regulated by the Prescription Drug Market Act of 1987. This requires drug companies to be factual and provide both benefits and risks with the drug.

Another form of marketing is switching products to be sold over the counter (OTC)—OTC drugs do not require a doctor's prescription. This usually happens after a patent has expired and the manufacturer is trying to capitalize and extend the life of a well-known brand. Prilosec, a heartburn treatment, is an example of a drug switched to OTC.

Off-Label Prescriptions   Once a drug is FDA approved for one indication (disease), doctors are allowed to prescribe the drug for any disease deemed appropriate. This "off-label" use of drug prescription is allowed in the US, but drug companies are only allowed to market a drug for its approved indication. It is estimated as much as 20 percent of all prescriptions are off-label, and this use can be a huge revenue driver for drug companies.

Generic Drugs

Generics are produced and sold without patent protection. They play a key role in drug prescriptions and lowering health care costs. Firms producing generics are generally product replicators, not innovators of new medicine. It is estimated generics account for over 60 percent of all prescriptions, yet account for less than 20 percent of total drug sales because of their lower cost.

Generic firms cannot charge premium pricing since their products have no unique characteristics. Instead, they must compete based on manufacturing and economies of scale. Many generic companies are domiciled in emerging markets, like Israel and India, where costs can be lower. Generic manufacturers may sell other products, like branded and OTC drugs, as a way to diversify and boost profitability since margins tend to be smaller and competition is fierce.

Generic firms can produce a drug when its patent expires, when the drug doesn't have a patent, when a country doesn't recognize the patent, or if it is able to prove in court the patent is either invalid or will not be infringed upon. When the manufacturer is ready to develop and sell the drug, it files an Abbreviated New Drug Application (ANDA) with the FDA for approval. Once approved, the generic is filed in the *orange book* (the FDA's list of approved medicines). The orange book lists both branded and generic drugs.

A generic drug must contain the same active ingredients as the branded version, and the manufacturer must only prove the drug is therapeutically equivalent to the branded one. Therefore, the company does not need to conduct clinical trials (which is why its FDA application is called "abbreviated"). Without the R&D costs, a generic drug's price can be significantly less than its branded counterpart's because the manufacturing cost of drugs is minimal (branded companies can achieve gross margins of 80 percent to 90 percent).

Patent Challenges   Challenging and invalidating patents can be a large part of a generic manufacturer's operation. According to the Hatch-Waxman Act, also known as the Drug Price Competition and Patent Term Restoration Act, a company that challenges and is first to file an ANDA against a branded drug's patent (known as a

Launching At-Risk

An at-risk launch is when a generic manufacturer challenges the validity of a patent and starts selling a generic version before the court rules on the case. Clearly, the reward for launching a generic drug is immense (due to the 180-day exclusivity). However, if the patent challenger ultimately loses the case, it may be "at risk" for treble damages. Treble damages means losing an at-risk launch in court may force the generic manufacturer to reimburse the branded company its lost sales, times a factor of three. An at-risk launch is dangerous, and the generic manufacturer should have the capacity to pay any possible damages. Table 5.7 lists the top 10 generic drug manufacturers.

Table 5.7   List of Generic Drug Makers

Rank	Company	Market Cap ($Mil)	Country
1	Teva	$46,132	Israel
2	Sun Pharmaceuticals	$6,056	India
3	Mylan	$5,090	US
4	Cipla	$5,489	India
5	Richter Gedeon	$4,096	Hungary
6	Watson Pharmaceuticals	$3,984	US
7	Ranbaxy Labs	$3,548	India
8	Perrigo	$3,451	US
9	Dr. Reddy's Laboratories	$3,431	India
10	Lupin	$2,382	India

Note: All companies may not be listed in the MSCI ACWI Managed Health Care Index.
Source: Bloomberg Finance, L.P., Thomson Reuters, MSCI, Inc.,[8] as of 12/31/2009.

paragraph IV challenge) is awarded 180 days of marketing exclusivity. The idea of the six-month exclusivity is to reward firms for the litigation risk they incur to challenge patents. The 180-day exclusivity is extremely profitable to the company that filed the ANDA because it essentially has no competition during that time—so it doesn't have to lower its price as much, increasing profits. Branded pharma companies may respond to the paragraph IV challenge and 180-day exclusivity period by contracting with another generic manufacturer to sell its branded drug at a lower price to compete with the generic. This is called an *authorized generic.*

Drug Industry Drivers

People want to live longer and healthier lives. Pretty basic. In that respect, the Health Care industry enjoys a higher fixed level of demand than just about any other industry. But that doesn't mean demand is static. There are several secular drivers playing a role in the drug industry, independent of the economic cycle.

Population Growth   The easiest long-term industry driver to diagnose is population growth—the more people, the more illnesses to combat. In this respect, the drug industry benefits from rising populations and purposefully seeks expansion in countries with the strongest population growth outlooks. Population growth may help drive longer term revenues and profits, but investors need to consider whether this will impact stock price returns over the next 12 to 18 months.

Increasing Wealth   The wealthier people are, the more health care they will consume (up to some limit, of course). This trend is taking shape in parts of the developing world, where demand has risen substantially simply because people can afford it. Economic gains are transforming societies at breakneck speeds in emerging markets and facilitating a rapid increase of the middle class in many countries. For example, the World Bank estimates that by 2030, more than 600 million people in East Asia will earn enough to be considered middle class, up from about 100 million in 2000. Along with increasing incomes, citizens of these countries are seeing higher standards of living, which positively impacts demand for better health products and services.

Demographic Shifts   Demographics are an important demand catalyst across the Health Care sector. As discussed in earlier chapters, aging populations generally consume more prescription drugs. Demographics are a longer-term driver, similar to population growth. However, investors should consider if or how this might impact near term stock price returns.

Innovation   For a branded drug company, innovation and new drug development are key to long-term success. If its pipeline is subpar, a company may engage in licensing agreements where it may develop and sell another company's products and collect a portion of the sales/ earnings. Another way of bolstering its pipeline is to buy another company with successful products and/or a promising pipeline.

Supply Drivers

Supply issues are generally less of a concern for small molecule firms (chemical pharmaceuticals). However, manufacturing large quantities of large molecule (biotech) drugs can be a challenge due to inherent complexities. A firm manufacturing drugs targeting specific diseases with little competition could be materially impacted if it is forced to delay or shut down operations due to a manufacturing glitch. A manufacturing delay can cause revenues and earnings to fall below expectations, which can then adversely impact the company's stock performance. From a generics standpoint, increased patent expirations could be supply drivers.

Access to Financing   Large drug firms tend to be very profitable and financially stable. Thus, access to financing generally isn't an issue. For example, during the market and liquidity crash of 2008, banks were very reluctant to lend, as evidenced by historically high credit spreads. However, big pharma was still able to access financing at favorable terms. Roche, Merck, and Pfizer were all able to secure financing to complete acquisitions.

While big bio-pharma can usually easily access credit, small drug companies with little to no revenues may find it very difficult to access capital. Many times these small drug companies have only pipeline candidates and regularly need multiple rounds of capital infusions to keep their research efforts in force. If capital liquidity dries up, these firms could go out of business. Companies with no marketed drugs and only pipeline candidates can be very risky because they generally aren't profitable and there is low probability of pipeline success—this tends to make their stock prices extremely volatile. For this reason, it is common for small firms to seek partnerships (licensing agreements or M&As) with big bio-pharma because they have the resources to finance drug development, manufacturing, and global distribution.

Regulation/Politics   Politics and regulation can have a tremendous impact on the drug industry. Please refer to Chapter 4 for a review on this topic.

The Life Sciences Industry

The overall global Life Sciences industry is valued around $60 billion and represents about 3 percent of the MSCI ACWI benchmark.[9.] Table 5.8 shows the 10 largest global Life Sciences companies, ranked by market capitalization.

Life Sciences firms support drug development by helping scientists perform qualitative and quantitative analysis to determine the molecular composition of a test sample. Qualitative data helps determine what it is, while quantitative data helps understand how much of it is there. Besides serving bio-pharma, Life Sciences companies' products and services are used to test air, food, and water quality and impurities in metals and consumer products (such as lead paint in toys). Its end markets are the drug industry, academic and government research labs, hospitals, and the industrial industry (which is an amalgamation of other industries served).

Table 5.8   Ten Largest Life Sciences Companies

Rank	Company	Market Cap ($Mil)	Country
1	Thermo Fisher Scientific	$19,346	US
2	Life Technologies	$8,577	US
3	Lonza Group	$5,672	Switzerland
4	Waters	$5,489	US
5	Illumina	$5,416	US
6	Qiagen	$5,010	Netherlands
7	Millipore	$3,978	US
8	Covance	$3,501	US
9	Mettler-Toledo	$3,144	Switzerland
10	Pharmaceutical Products Development	$2,677	US

Note: All companies may not be listed in the MSCI ACWI Managed Health Care Index.
Source: Bloomberg Finance, L.P., Thomson Reuters, MSCI, Inc.[10] as of 12/31/2009.

Life Sciences firms generally sell three types of products: (1) instruments, (2) consumables, and (3) software. Bio-pharma may also outsource R&D activities to Life Sciences companies—this is known as a contract research organization (CRO). CROs can often conduct trials and collect data more efficiently than the drug company itself.

Instruments are usually the equipment used to perform the test. Instrument costs can range from inexpensive to large capital outlays. Broader economic activity can influence equipment sales because of the costs associated with some instruments—organizations may try to limit capital outlays when times are tough. Examples of equipment are chromatography machines, which are used to separate mixtures in order to determine their components, and robotic systems to handle test samples on a large scale.

Consumables range from disposable laboratory glassware, tubes, and vials, to chemicals, reagents, and organisms used in large molecule research. Compared to instruments, consumables tend to have relatively more stable demand. One can think of instruments and consumables like a razor and razor blades. The razor is the piece of equipment while the razor blades are the consumables.

Software is usually a smaller part of revenues. Usually the software is used to automate, analyze, and manage data. The software can be used in conjunction with the equipment.

Life Sciences Industry Drivers

The Life Sciences industry is influenced by many factors. Some of the more important drivers are R&D expenditures, government spending, economic activity, and distribution.

R&D   Bio-pharma and academic/government R&D activities can be a significant portion of the Life Sciences industry's revenues. Therefore, it is important to track R&D trends—are they generally rising or falling? As mentioned previously, bio-pharma R&D is usually reflected as a percentage of its sales. If sales are generally falling, then this could be one indication R&D expenses may remain flat or decline.

Government Spending   Academic/government R&D is driven by government funding, particularly from the National Institutes of Health (NIH) in the United States. The NIH is a federal agency conducting and supporting medical research. Demand for Life Sciences could be greater than expected if the NIH budget grows faster than expected. If the president of the United States urges an increase in research funding, it generally bodes well for the Life Sciences industry. The NIH website (www.NIH.gov) is full of useful information, including its budget (about $30 billion) and how funds are spent. Following its budget and comparing it to consensus expectations can help give investors an idea of whether the Life Sciences industry will outperform or underperform.

Economic Activity   As mentioned earlier, the Life Sciences industry tends to be more economically sensitive than the drug industry. When times are good, industrial firms and hospitals may increase their capital expenditures and buy new equipment. The opposite occurs during an economic contraction, and companies, including hospitals, tighten their budgets.

Distribution   It is important to understand how a company distributes its products. In particular, many Life Sciences firms derive a significant portion of their revenues from non-US sources. Therefore, understanding currency movements is critical because a rising dollar, all else being equal, lowers demand for US products. Currency movements can materially impact operations and share price performance.

HEALTH CARE EQUIPMENT & SERVICES INDUSTRY GROUP

The Health Care Equipment & Services industry group is broken down into three industries and seven sub-industries:

1. Health Care Equipment & Supplies
   i. Health Care Equipment
   ii. Health Care Supplies
2. Health Care Providers & Services
   iii. Health Care Distributors
   iv. Health Care Facilities
   v. Health Care Services
   vi. Managed Health Care
3. Health Care Technology
   vii. Health Care Technology

This group has a diverse set of offerings. Equipment, Supplies, and Distributors are self explanatory. Facilities represents hospitals, rehabilitation centers, and nursing homes. Services companies include laboratory testing and pharmacy benefit managers. Health Care Technology provides information technology like electronic health records to health care providers.

Health Care Equipment & Supplies

The Health Care Equipment & Supplies industry is broken into two distinct categories:

1. **Health Care Equipment.** Manufacturers of health care equipment and devices like furniture, artificial joints, and X-ray machines.

2. Health Care Supplies. Manufacturers of general supplies found in hospitals and doctor's offices. These products include items like rubber gloves, masks, and syringes.

Many companies offer equipment and supplies, and the drivers are similar, so both will be discussed together as Health Care Equipment.

Health Care Equipment   The market capitalization of equipment makers is nearly $300 billion,[11] making it the second largest sub-industry within the Health Care sector. Table 5.9 shows the 10 largest stand-alone equipment makers by market capitalization. Not included are subsidiaries of other companies, including Johnson & Johnson, General Electric, Siemens, and Philips. If independent, the divisions of these four firms would be listed among the largest equipment companies.

The Health Care Equipment sub-industry is highly diverse, manufacturing and selling thousands of products. Equipment costs can require large capital outlays or they can be relatively inexpensive. Equipment can be divided into two categories: conventional and high tech.

Conventional products, such as trays, tables, scalpels, and furniture, tend to be a low-margin, high-volume business. These products

Table 5.9   Ten Largest Global Health Care Equipment Firms

Rank	Company	Market Cap ($Mil)	Country
1	Medtronic	$48,583	US
2	Baxter International	$35,376	US
3	Covidien	$24,062	Ireland
4	Stryker	$20,034	US
5	Becton Dickinson	$18,587	US
6	Synthes	$15,539	Switzerland
7	Boston Scientific	$13,594	US
8	St. Jude Medical	$12,294	US
9	Zimmer Holdings	$12,589	US
10	Intuitive Surgical	$11,589	US

Note: All companies may not be listed in the MSCI ACWI Managed Health Care Index.
Source: Bloomberg Finance, L.P., Thomson Reuters, MSCI, Inc.,[12] as of 12/31/2009.

are generally sold on a contract basis to group purchasing organizations (GPOs). GPOs represent hospitals and physicians to obtain discount pricing through bulk purchases. Conventional product sales and cash flows tend to be fairly consistent.

High-tech products are more advanced devices, and differentiated products can generate high margins. High-tech devices require substantial R&D funding. Examples of high-tech products include drug-eluting stents and implantable cardiovascular devices. Equipment makers sell their products to hospitals and doctors, who, in turn, are reimbursed by insurance and government agencies. GPOs have less influence over high-tech product pricing because surgeons and doctors may prefer a particular company's product.

Frequently, a firm will offer a broad array of medical equipment and supplies. The steady revenue and cash flows from low-tech products can help fund R&D costs for high-tech products. Similar to the drug industry, it is common for large and small firms to depend upon each other for success—small firms innovate niche products, and large firms have the means to develop, manufacture, market, and distribute them.

Competition is fierce and innovation can render high-tech products and inventory obsolete. Companies are less reliant upon patents for success, partially because next-generation devices are quickly developed and partially because equipment patents are not as strong as drug patents. While drug companies can have sales exclusivity for 10 or more years, equipment companies may only have exclusivity for 1 or 2 years.

Major Equipment Markets High-tech equipment is generally used in cardiology, orthopedics, diagnostic imaging, and in vitro diagnostics.

Cardiovascular equipment addresses the heart and blood vessels, and includes pacemakers and defibrillators, stents, and cardiac valves. Pacemakers and defibrillators help regulate the patient's heart rhythm. These can be implanted in the chest or worn externally. A stent is a tube used to open arteries to allow proper blood flow. Artificial heart valves replace dysfunctional heart valves, which help regulate blood flow between the heart chambers. The major players in this market include Abbott Labs, Boston Scientific, Johnson & Johnson, Medtronic, and St. Jude.

Orthopedics deals with the skeletal system, which includes artificial knees, joints, hips, shoulders, and spine. Osteoarthritis (degradation of joints), rheumatoid arthritis (degradation of cartilage around joints), and injuries from sports and auto accidents are common reasons patients see an orthopedic surgeon. The major orthopedic players include Johnson & Johnson, Medtronic, Stryker, and Zimmer.

Diagnostic imaging creates images of the body in order to diagnose a certain condition. These include X-rays, magnetic resonance imaging (MRI), computed tomography (CT), and ultrasound imaging. Major players include General Electric, Siemens, and Philips.

In vitro diagnostics test the blood, tissue, and other bodily fluids for disease. Diagnostics consist of reagents (reactants) and equipment used to analyze how the reagent mixes with the test subject (blood, fluid, etc). Pharmaceutical and Life Sciences companies can offer diagnostic equipment. The major players include Roche, Siemens, Abbott Labs, and Johnson & Johnson.

Regulation and the Approval Process   In the US, the FDA is responsible for product approval and patient safety. Japan, the EU, and Australia have regulatory bodies similar to the FDA, with similar approval requirements. Some countries, particularly emerging countries, have little to no regulatory oversight. In most developed nations, equipment firms must provide extensive research and documentation to get their products approved.

When a device is submitted to the FDA for approval, it falls into one of three classes based on risk perception.

- **Class 1.** Products that pose a low degree of risk to the patient, like a stethoscope and other low-tech supplies. A company must notify the FDA 90 days beforehand that it will sell these products and demonstrate that its manufacturing practices are sound.

- **Class 2.** Products that pose a moderate degree of risk to the patient, such as an X-ray machine. Companies must provide evidence of safety and manufacturing soundness.
- **Class 3.** Complex products that pose a high degree of risk to the patient, such as an implantable pacemaker. These products generally support life or prevent life-threatening events like a stroke from happening.

Device manufacturers must file either a premarket notification or a premarket application with the FDA before the product can be approved for marketing. An investigational device exemption (IDE) must be filed to conduct human clinical trials. A premarket notification, known as a 510(k), is filed for products similar to other products already on the market and must compare safety and effectiveness between the two. A premarket application is filed for new products without similarly marketed products. This application must show clinical trial results and is generally more robust and time consuming than a premarket notification. Medical devices need a *Conformité Européene* (CE) mark before they can be marketed in the EU. A CE mark indicates a product meets safety and performance standards.

Health Care Equipment Drivers

The Health Care Equipment sub-industry is influenced by many factors. Some of the more important drivers are innovation, demographics, legislation and regulation, government expenditures, economic activity, price, and foreign markets.

Innovation   High-tech equipment firms are constantly in search of innovative new products. New and better products garner pricing power and high margins; therefore, companies constantly need new products to grow the top and bottom lines. Equipment firms often work with physicians to update and enhance existing products. Innovators sometimes approach larger firms to develop and sell their products, while other times, one firm will acquire another for its pipeline.

Demographics As with most Health Care industries, demographics play an important role in equipment demand. In general, older people tend to demand more heart valves, pacemakers, and artificial joints. Therefore, it's important to understand a company's customer base. An aging population may be a longer-term revenue and earnings driver, but one should also consider how this factor may influence share price performance over the next 12 to 18 months.

Legislation/Regulation Legislation may increase or decrease taxes or fees, while regulation may make it harder or easier to operate in a particular industry. The FDA may be more or less strict. Following legislative and regulatory developments is very important because they can have material consequences for an industry.

Government Expenditures Medicare and Medicaid reimburse hospitals and doctors in amounts determined by certain codes. For their products to thrive, it's important for manufacturers to obtain favorable reimbursement rates. A government may also change its reimbursement rate for certain products, which may influence a firm's pricing, revenues, and profits.

Economic Activity Elective surgeries tend to be relatively more economically sensitive. When times are good, companies may buy the newest high-tech machine, and people may choose to have their knee replaced or have plastic surgery. Purse strings tend to tighten during an economic contraction, and some equipment makers feel the pinch.

Price Like other products, pricing is very important and can be influenced by several factors. High-tech products with little competition can command premium pricing, while increasing competition generally lowers pricing power. Governments, insurance companies, and group purchasing organizations are constantly trying to reduce health costs and try to pressure pricing as well.

Foreign Markets   Large companies can garner 50 percent or more of sales from non-domestic sources. Foreign markets, particularly developing markets, are experiencing faster growth as an increase in wealth is spurring demand for higher quality medical care. Foreign currency fluctuations are important to monitor because they can make domestic goods appear cheaper or more expensive, therefore influencing revenues, costs, and profits.

Health Care Supplies

The market capitalization of the Health Care Supplies sub-industry is $22 billion, less than 1 percent of the MSCI ACWI Health Care Index.[13] The size of the Health Care Supplies market is significantly smaller than its Equipment counterpart. The largest Supplies companies are listed in Table 5.10.

The operating environment and drivers are similar to the equipment makers, and the two sub-industries often overlap (i.e., one firm will offer both types of products). For that reason, a description of industry operations and drivers will not be discussed again. Remember, supplies are typically lower-margin, commodity-type products sold on a contract basis. Revenues tend to be relatively stable.

Table 5.10   Ten Largest Health Care Supplies Firms

Rank	Company	Market Cap ($Mil)	Country
1	Alcon	$49,231	Switzerland
2	Essilor	$12,603	France
3	Dentsply	$5,223	US
4	Coloplast	$3,776	Denmark
5	Inverness	$3,454	US
6	SSL International	$2,694	UK
7	Shandong Weig	$1,430	China
8	Haemonetics	$1,386	US
9	Nipro Corp	$1,317	Japan
10	West Pharmaceuticals	$1,294	US

Note: All companies may not be listed in the MSCI ACWI Managed Health Care Index.
Source: Bloomberg Finance, L.P., Thomson Reuters, MSCI Inc.,[14] as of 12/31/2009.

HEALTH CARE PROVIDERS & SERVICES

Providers & Services firms offer a diverse range of products that are primarily service-based, and they sell to individuals and other companies. The industry is broken down into four sub-industries: Distributors, Facilities, Managed Care, and Services.

Health Care Distributors

The market capitalization of the Health Care Distributors sub-industry is roughly $54 billion, representing about 2.5 percent of the MSCI ACWI Health Care Index.[15] Table 5.11 shows the world's largest distributors, based on market cap.

Distributors buy prescription drugs, medical equipment, information technology, and other products from manufacturers and sell them to pharmacies, hospitals, veterinarians, and physicians across the country. They make sure products get to end markets. Distribution centers and logistics help customers maintain timely and appropriate inventory levels.

Distributors are generally paid on a fee-for-service or buy-and-hold contract. A fee-for-service contract generally earns distributors a percentage of the amount of product they sell. A buy-and-hold

Table 5.11   Ten Largest Health Care Distribution Companies

Rank	Company	Market Cap ($Mil)	Country
1	McKessen	$16,837	US
2	Cardinal Health	$11,693	US
3	AmerisourceBergen	$7,510	US
4	Henry Schein	$4,759	US
5	Celesio	$4,344	Germany
6	Patterson	$3,427	US
7	Suzuken	$3,078	Japan
8	Medipal	$3,023	Japan
9	Sinopharm	$2,453	China
10	Galenica	$2,358	Switzerland

Note: All companies may not be listed in the MSCI ACWI Managed Health Care Index.
Source: Bloomberg Finance, L.P., Thomson Reuters, MSCI, Inc.,[16] as of 12/31/2009.

strategy allows customers to buy products ahead of orders, hold products, and benefit when product prices increase in value. Generally, the industry is transitioning away from buy-and-hold and toward the percentage-based program because it tends to produce steadier sales results.

Distributor Drivers

The Health Care Distributors sub-industry is influenced by many factors. Some of the more important drivers are volume, cost control, and generic drugs.

Volume

Volume is critical because it drives revenue growth and scale. Volume can be driven by higher utilization, more written prescriptions per person, or more participants being covered by insurance.

Cost Control

Operating margins for distributors can be in the low single digits; therefore, inventory management and cost containment are major drivers of earnings performance. Small percentage changes in revenues and expenses can materially impact bottom line results.

Generic Drugs

Generic drug distribution provides an opportunity to grow margins because distributors have better negotiating power due to competition among generic manufacturers and their heavy reliance upon distributors to sell their products.

HEALTH CARE FACILITIES

The market capitalization of the Health Care Facilities sub-industry is roughly $2 billion.[17] It's the smallest industry, representing 0.1 percent of the MSCI ACWI Health Care Index. Table 5.12 lists the

Table 5.12   Ten Largest Health Care Facilities Companies

Rank	Company	Market Cap ($Mil)	Country
1	Rhoen-Klinikum	$3,385	Germany
2	Community Health System	$3,309	US
3	Universal Health Services	$2,777	US
4	Netcare	$2,675	South Africa
5	Tenet Healthcare	$2,593	US
6	Parkway Holdings	$2,351	Singapore
7	Brookdale Senior Living	$2,158	US
8	VCA Antech	$2,130	US
9	Ramsay Health Care	$1,979	Australia
10	Health Management Association	$1,806	US

Note: All companies may not be listed in the MSCI ACWI Managed Health Care Index.
Source: Bloomberg Finance, L.P., Thomson Reuters, MSCI, Inc.,[18] as of 12/31/2009.

world's largest Health Care Facilities, based on market cap. The sub-industry is highly fragmented—we won't spend much time detailing it because the sub-industry is so tiny, its performance little impacts the overall sector, and you can spend your time more profitably elsewhere.

Health Care Facilities includes many types of operations, with the primary ones being acute care hospitals, rehabilitation centers, psychiatric hospitals, nursing homes, assisted-living facilities, and home health care services.

HEALTH CARE SERVICES

The market capitalization of the Health Care Services sub-industry is roughly $95 billion, representing 4 percent of the MSCI ACWI Health Care Index.[19] Table 5.13 shows the world's largest Health Care Services firms, based on market cap.

Health Care Services firms include pharmacy benefit managers, laboratory testing services, dialysis centers, contract research organizations, and more. Each type of business is fairly unique. However, this section will focus on pharmacy benefit managers (PBMs) since they dominate the Services sub-industry.

Table 5.13   Ten Largest Health Care Services Firms

Rank	Company	Market Cap ($Mil)	Country
1	Medco Health Solutions	$30,470	US
2	Express Scripts	$23,741	US
3	Fresenius Medical Care	$15,612	Germany
4	Quest Diagnostics	$11,164	US
5	Laboratory Corp of America	$7,948	US
6	Davita	$6,003	US
7	Sonic Healthcare	$5,369	Australia
8	Omnicare	$2,886	US
9	Mednax	$2,797	US
10	Primary Health	$2,588	Australia

Note: All companies may not be listed in the MSCI ACWI Managed Health Care Index.
Source: Bloomberg Finance, L.P., Thomson Reuters, MSCI, Inc.,[20] as of 12/31/2009.

Pharmacy Benefit Manager

PBMs are third-party administrators of prescription drugs, but they don't actually take possession of the drugs. Instead, they manage drug programs for plan sponsors (health insurance companies, employers, etc.) by processing and paying drug claims. PBMs also develop and maintain the formulary list. They coordinate activities between drug manufacturers, pharmacies, and plan sponsors.

Because they work for plan sponsors, PBMs aim to lower the cost of drugs. PBMs represent millions of members, so they can achieve lower prices by contracting and negotiating discounts with drug manufacturers and pharmacies. In return, manufacturers and pharmacies gain access to a greater number of customers. Another way to lower drug costs is by monitoring doctor prescriptions and suggesting lower-cost generic drugs when appropriate.

PBMs generate revenues from manufacturers, pharmacies, and plan sponsors. Drug manufacturers provide PBMs rebates (for favorable formulary position and market share) and pay administrative fees to access data on prescription trends and utilization. A portion of the rebates are passed on to plan sponsors, and PBMs keep the spread. Pharmacies may pay PBMs to be included in the network. Plan sponsors pay PBMs administrative fees to manage the drug program.

Putting It All Together   Using our friend Shane the Patient from Chapter 1 (and assuming he's covered by a prescription drug plan), let's walk through an example of how PBMs operate.

After his stroke, Shane's doctor prescribed him several drugs, and Shane went to a pharmacy to have the prescriptions filled. The pharmacist checked with the PBM to determine whether the prescribed drug is on the formulary list—the list tells the pharmacist whether Shane has a co-pay, and if so, how much. The PBM approved the drug, paid the pharmacy, and Shane got his medicine. Afterward, the plan sponsor reimbursed the PBM for the cost of Shane's prescription. If the doctor prescribed an expensive branded drug, the PBM may suggest a preferred branded drug (tier two) or a generic version (tier one), if available, to lower the cost.

PBM Drivers

PBMs are influenced by drivers similar to distributors, namely volume and demand for generic drugs, but developing a network is vitally important as well.

Volume   Increased demand comes from more people being covered by a prescription drug plan. In addition, increased prescriptions per person also raise demand. Many times, as people age, more prescriptions are needed per person.

Generic Drugs and Mail-Order Pharmacy   Similar to Health Care Distributors, PBMs obtain greater bargaining power and higher margins through generic drugs. Additionally, mail-order pharmacies generate higher margins since they are able to automate the process, control prescription administration, and work in large bulk supply. A mail order pharmacy is a PBM-owned dispensing facility where drug refills are sent to the patient through the mail. Refills sent by a mail-order pharmacy are usually 90-day supplies instead of the typical 30 days dispensed by regular pharmacies.

Network Development   Developing the network is paramount to developing economies of scale. A PBM must administer many drug plans and represent many people in order to negotiate larger discounts. On the other side, the network must include manufacturers and pharmacies to provide the patient with products.

MANAGED HEALTH CARE

The market capitalization of the Managed Health Care sub-industry is roughly $82 billion, representing 3.5 percent of the MSCI ACWI Health Care Index.[21] Table 5.14 shows the world's largest Managed Health Care firms, based on market cap.

Managed Health Care is the health insurance industry. From a market cap standpoint, the vast majority of health insurers are US-based because there is little room for private industry in a government-run universal health care system. Therefore, the discussion on health insurers will center on the US system. There are private health insurance companies in other countries, but they typically sell policies that supplement the government's insurance.

Health insurance firms, like other insurance firms, are in the business of risk management. Customers (aka members) pay premiums to

Table 5.14   Ten Largest Managed Health Care Firms

Rank	Company	Market Cap ($Mil)	Country
1	United Health	$35,418	US
2	WellPoint	$26,717	US
3	Aetna	$13,742	US
4	Cigna	$9,644	US
5	Humana	$7,454	US
6	Coventry	$3,595	US
7	Health Net	$2,421	US
8	Odontoprev S.A.	$1,625	Brazil
9	Wellcare Group	$1,070	US
10	Amerigroup	$1,180	US

Note: All companies may not be listed in the MSCI ACWI Managed Health Care Index.
Source: Bloomberg Finance, L.P., Thomson Reuters, MSCI, Inc.,[22] as of 12/31/2009.

an insurance firm to assume the risk of monetary loss. Policy pricing is based upon a myriad of factors like age, frequency of illness and hospital utilization trends, and a host of other statistical probabilities. Insurance firms have large investment portfolios because they invest premiums received. Investment portfolios not only generate revenue, but the investment income may also factor into policy pricing. Simply, a company's profit is determined by adding premiums and investment income and subtracting benefit payments, underwriting, and operating expenses.

Health insurers sell to individuals, the government, the commercial market, or all of the above. Insurance companies employ a sales force to sell policies to all end markets. Government insurance covers Medicare (the elderly), Medicaid (the poor), military, SCHIP (State Children's Health Insurance Program), and government employees. Commercial insurance is where many people obtain their coverage—through work. Individuals not covered through their employer may buy individual policies. (Reference Chapter 2 for a detailed description of the types of insurance plans available.)

Health insurance is regulated at the state, not federal, level. Moreover, the industry is exempt from federal antitrust legislation by way of the McCarran-Ferguson Act. Health insurance plans cannot compete across state lines, and some insurance firms have a monopoly in some states or counties. Since insurance is regulated at the state level and intrastate competition is not allowed, large insurance firms operate as holding companies, with subsidiaries operating in each state.

The industry, although consolidating, remains relatively fragmented. Nonprofit and profit-driven companies are prevalent. With over 100 million members, Blue Cross Blue Shield is the largest managed care organization in the US. Blue Cross is an association of independently operated plans throughout the US—some are nonprofit while some are for profit. Profit-driven firms have been consolidating over the years to drive scale amid heavy competition. WellPoint and UnitedHealth are the largest for-profit firms with about 30 million members each.

Managed Care Drivers

The Managed Care sub-industry can be impacted by a myriad of factors. Some of the more important factors that can impact operational and share price performance include membership growth, policy pricing, cost control, actuary ability, investment portfolio performance, government expenditures, and legislative changes.

Membership Growth

Membership growth is important—it can grow revenues and profits. The economy can impact membership because higher employment levels increase insurance coverage. The opposite happens when companies downsize.

Pricing

Like with most products, pricing is very important. However, when pricing a policy, an insurance company must consider not only its competitors' prices, but also expected patient utilization and medical inflation rates.

Cost Control

Managing costs is at the heart of the industry, and the two major costs a health insurance company incurs are medical benefits and selling, general, and administrative expenses (SG&A). A closely watched statistic is a company's medical loss ratio (MLR), also known as the medical cost ratio (MCR). This ratio represents benefits paid divided by premiums earned. Generally, the ratio is in the high 70 percent to mid-80 percent range. An MLR of 82 percent means that for every dollar of premium brought in, 82 cents was spent on medical claims. SG&A as a percent of revenues can run 10 to 15 percent. Medical and SG&A costs generally leave operating profit margins in the single digits, and an MLR slightly higher or lower than expectations can have a material impact on profits.

Actuary Ability

The actuary estimates costs and probabilities, which impacts pricing and profitability. At the end of a reporting period, a company closes its books while member activity is ongoing. Therefore, a company must estimate its full period expense because all claims during the quarter have not been received. This is called the incurred but not reported expense (IBNR), one of the major expenses a health insurance actuary must estimate. Accurate IBNR expense estimates require skill and analysis, and actuarial abilities impact company profits and investor sentiment. IBNR expense is reported as a reserve liability on the balance sheet as part of medical claims payable. A company may "release reserves" if it realizes it over-reserved expenses in a period, which positively impacts the following period's earnings. This is also known as a positive prior period development.

Investment Portfolio Performance

A health insurance company's investment portfolio helps drive revenue, earnings, and policy pricing. If the portfolio is performing well, the company can price policies relatively well because any potential losses can be compensated by the portfolio gains. However, during an economic downturn, the portfolio may experience investment losses, pressuring earnings and balance sheet strength and resulting in higher policy premiums.

Government Expenditures

Government reimbursements can materially impact firm profitability. An insurance firm's share price can materially move when the government announces its reimbursement rates.

Legislative Changes

Legislation can cause a tremendous amount of uncertainty. Take the 2009 health care reform debates, for example. Some argued universal coverage or a government-run insurance company could wipe out the

Days Claims Payable

Investors use the days claims payable (DCP) ratio to assess earnings quality. DCP is medical claims payable divided by the average daily medical expense. This tells you how many days it would take to pay all outstanding medical claims.

$$DCP = \frac{Medical\ claims\ payable}{Medical\ expense/days\ in\ period}$$

Small changes in the number can have a material impact on earnings. In general, a declining DCP ratio is a warning sign because it can lead to weaker earnings quality. An increasing DCP ratio means the company is conservatively reserving for future medical expenses.

entire industry. Other potential measures, such as expanding coverage to all citizens and minimum MLRs, raise questions about future profitability.

HEALTH CARE TECHNOLOGY

The market capitalization of the Health Care Technology sub-industry is roughly $9 billion, representing 0.4 percent of the MSCI ACWI Health Care Index.[23] Table 5.15 shows the world's largest Health Care Tech firms, based on market cap.

Health Care Technology is a relatively new field and deals with the information technology side of the Health Care industry. Firms include those gathering and processing data to those providing software for scheduling doctor's appointments, creating electronic health records, billing and payment collection, and managing drug prescriptions. The industry's target markets are commercial businesses (e.g., hospitals, doctors' offices, etc.) and the government. This industry can be more sensitive to economic activity since health care technology is generally a capital equipment type of purchase.

Table 5.15   Ten Largest Health Care Technology Companies

Rank	Company	Market Cap ($Mil)	Country
1	Cerner Corp	$6,730	US
2	Allscripts-Mysis	$2,936	US
3	Quality Systems	$1,799	US
4	SXC Health Solutions	$1,621	US
5	AthenaHealth Inc.	$1,524	US
6	Medasets Inc.	$1,200	US
7	Cegedim SA	$1,155	France
8	Eclipsys Corp	$1,055	US
9	So-Net M3	$793	Japan
10	Isoft Grop	$719	Australia

Note: Not all companies are listed in the MSCI ACWI Health Care Technology Index.
Source: Bloomberg Finance, L.P., Thomson Reuters, MSCI, Inc.,[24] as of 12/31/2009.

This segment is very small relative to the other industries, but it is growing quickly and has a lot of potential. Although the practice of medicine is highly advanced, the operational side of health care delivery and record retention is archaic and cumbersome. Many doctors still use paper files and handwrite prescriptions. Various hospital departments don't have the proper technology to communicate with each other effectively. Additionally, there is no common communication system among insurance companies, doctors, and patients—this helps explain why billing and payments are so incredibly complicated for everyone involved.

Chapter 1 listed inefficient claims processing and use of technology as major contributors to wasted health care spending, and innovative information technology has the ability to address this issue. Desire for efficiency is the sub-industry's primary driver. Government support to encourage technology adoption is also driving demand. However, patient privacy, high cost, time commitment required to learn new programs, and lack of a common technological platform are major obstacles that need to be addressed.

Chapter Recap

- The Health Care sector is comprised of a variety of sub-industries, including Pharmaceuticals, Biotechnology, Life Sciences, Equipment, Supplies, Distributors, Services, Facilities, Managed Health Care, and Technology. While most sub-industries possess similar inelastic demand characteristics, each also possesses unique operating environments and drivers.

- The drug industry includes Pharmaceuticals and Biotechnology companies. Pharmaceutical drugs are small molecule drugs made of chemicals. Biotechnology drugs are large molecule drugs made of live organisms. The drug industry is a high-risk, high-reward business. It is costly and takes years to bring a drug to market—the industry is highly regulated.

- Drivers of the drug industry include population growth, wealth, demographic shifts, foreign markets, innovation, and regulatory and legislative development.

- The Life Sciences sub-industry supports the drug industry, academic and government research labs, hospitals, and the industrial industry by providing qualitative and quantitative data on test samples. Qualitative data determine what's in the sample, and quantitative data determine how much of it is in there.

- Drivers of the Life Sciences sub-industry include bio-pharmaceutical R&D spending, government spending, global distribution, and economic activity.

- The Health Care Equipment & Supplies industry manufactures and distributes high-tech and low-tech products. High-tech products are differentiated, higher-margin products used to treat the heart, spine, bones, and other parts of the body. Low-tech, low-margin, conventional products include tables, furniture, scalpels, gloves, and clothing. Many companies sell both types of products. Equipment is regulated by the FDA.

- Drivers of the Health Care Equipment & Supplies industry include innovation, demographics, wealth, government spending, regulation, and pricing/competition.

- The Health Care Distributors sub-industry is responsible for bringing drugs, equipment, software, and other products to hospitals, pharmacies, and physicians' offices.

- Drivers of the Distributors sub-industry include volume growth, generic drugs, and cost control.

- The Health Care Facilities sub-industry includes many types of operations, with the primary ones being acute care hospitals, rehabilitation centers, psychiatric hospitals, nursing homes, assisted-living facilities, and home health care services. Facilities can be nonprofit or profit-driven organizations.

- Drivers of the Facilities sub-industry include admission and population growth, economic growth, government spending, and regulatory changes.
- The Health Care Services sub-industry comprises several types of businesses, including PBMs, laboratory testing services, dialysis centers, and contract research organizations. Each type of business has unique characteristics. PBMs dominate the services industry.
- PBM drivers include networks, generic drugs, increased numbers of people covered by a prescription drug plan, and prescriptions-per-person growth.
- Managed Care is the health insurance industry. From a market cap standpoint, the vast majority of health insurers are US-based because governments in most other developed countries pay for health care. There are several types of insurance plans, including HMOs, PPOs, POS and consumer-directed plans, and Medicare Advantage. Managed Care organizations also administer Medicare and Medicaid.
- Managed Care drivers include membership growth, pricing, actuary abilities, economic activity, investment portfolio performance, government spending, cost control, and legislation.
- Health Care Technology is a relatively new field and deals with the information technology side of health care. The industry includes different types of companies, ranging from firms gathering and processing data to companies providing software for scheduling doctors' appointments, creating electronic health records, billing and collecting payments, and prescribing drugs.
- Drivers of the Health Care Technology sub-industry include government support and the willingness and ability of providers to encourage change.

6

CHALLENGES IN THE HEALTH CARE SECTOR

In addition to understanding the sector composition and drivers, it's important to understand the sector's challenges and the risks those challenges pose to near and longer-term growth prospects. Health Care has traditionally been a growth industry as demand, innovation, and pricing power led the sector to grow faster than the general economy. Recently, many firms (particularly in the Pharmaceuticals industry) have begun to lose the premium valuations generally associated with growth stocks and are looking more like value stocks as they address several pressing issues. However, neither growth nor value characteristics are inherently better or worse than the other. Here, we focus on three challenges specific to Health Care: slowing growth in mature markets, innovation, and regulation and legislation.

This chapter also discusses ways firms address these challenges, including pipeline development and licensing agreements, acquisitions, and restructuring. When doing a sector analysis, identifying opportunities is just half the battle. Understanding how management responds to challenges should help you judge a company's efficiency, future prospects, valuations, and overall attractiveness.

SLOWING GROWTH IN MATURE MARKETS

Companies and industries cannot grow quickly all the time. Many large Health Care companies, particularly Pharmaceuticals, are finding it relatively challenging to grow revenues and earnings in markets where they are well established. Factors contributing to slow growth in mature markets include:

- Patent expirations
- Competition from innovators and generic manufacturers
- Pricing pressures
- Weak pipelines

Patent Expirations

One of the major challenges facing the Pharmaceuticals industry is the "patent cliff." It's estimated $140 billion worth of branded drug sales (nearly 20 percent of 2009 global drug sales) will lose patent protection from 2009 through 2013.[1] Remember, sales of the original branded drug can decline as much as 80 percent or more after a patent expires and generics start competing. Many of the world's largest branded pharmaceutical drugs will lose patent exclusivity over this time frame, causing some firms to lose as much as 50 percent or more of their total revenues.

For example, between 2010 and 2014, AstraZeneca is expected to lose patent protection on Nexium (heartburn), Seroquel (bipolar disorder), Symbicort (asthma), Arimidex (breast cancer), Atacand (blood pressure), Zoladex (prostate/breast cancer), and Merrem I.V. (bacterial infection).[2] Combined, these drugs represent over 50 percent of the firm's 2008 sales. It is very difficult for a company to offset losses of this magnitude, let alone grow sales and earnings. After all, Health Care firms cannot rely solely on a rebounding economy to increase sales, unlike economically sensitive firms (which can to some degree).

Competition From Innovators and Generic Manufacturers

Competition from both innovators and generics puts pressure on pricing and profitability. Competition among innovators impacts pricing in nearly all industries—Health Care is no different. Plus, innovation in medical equipment happens so quickly, it can render relatively new innovations obsolete in no time.

Generic drug makers actively seek to invalidate branded drug patents because it's highly profitable—for them. Therefore, branded drugs can lose sales exclusivity well before the patent expires. Branded competitors are impacted as well because doctors and patients in the US tend to favor generics. If available, patients starting a new treatment may be prescribed a generic, or patients taking a branded competitor may switch to a generic counterpart. For example, US sales of Pfizer's Lipitor have been impacted ever since the patent for Merck's Zocor—a similar drug—expired in 2006.

Apotex, a Canadian generic manufacturer, is an example of how patent challenges can impact sales of a branded drug.

In 2006, Apotex launched a generic version of Plavix, a blood thinner co-marketed by Sanofi-Aventis and Bristol Myers Squibb. Plavix is the world's second best-selling drug, behind Pfizer's cholesterol drug Lipitor. Apotex decided to launch the generic version "at risk." Bristol Myers failed to settle the matter with Apotex out of court, which would have prevented Apotex from selling the generic version. Eventually, the court ruled in favor of Bristol and demanded Apotex cease sales of the generic version, but not before Apotex was able to sell several months worth of product. Management estimated the generic negatively impacted 2006 sales of Plavix by $1.2 to $1.4 billion.[3]

Pricing Pressures

Health care costs are a major concern globally, and all major payers of health care are trying to slow the rate of growth—governments and insurance companies are constantly trying to negotiate lower contracts, reduce reimbursements, or increase rebates. In countries where the government is the primary payer for medical services, the government wields material buying power and sometimes forces medical companies to make price concessions. For example, the Japanese government orders price cuts on prescription drugs every two years. In 2008, the cuts averaged about 5 percent.[4] Prior years have been higher and lower. Additionally, Group Purchasing Organizations (GPOs) and Pharmacy Benefit Managers (PBMs) attempt the same as they negotiate lower prices for their customers.

Pricing pressure also comes from competitive forces, including drug reimportation. Drug reimportation occurs when a company sells its drugs in another country at lower prices than it does domestically. In turn, domestic customers purchase the drugs from the country with the lower prices. Drug reimportation is currently illegal in the US, but legislators seriously considered legalizing it during the 2009 health care reform debate as a way to lower costs. It's possible they will consider it again in the future. And remember: Heavy government involvement in the Health Care sector has helped drive material pricing distortions around the world.

Weak Pipelines

Another major challenge is that many Pharmaceuticals firms now are considered to have weak pipelines—that is their pipelines of new drugs aren't expected to have enough new product launches to make up for upcoming patent expirations. If a firm's total annual revenues are $20 billion, and 50 percent of its sales lose patent exclusivity over the next few years, its pipeline must deliver roughly $10 billion of new revenue sources just to keep sales steady. Remember, only about 1 in 5,000 compounds ever makes it to market, and fewer than one third of marketed drugs are profitable. Additionally, it takes time to ramp up sales of a new product because doctors, patients, and payers need to get comfortable with it. So if a company has five drugs in Phase III development, it will be very challenging for the company to maintain sales over its patent cliff period.

AstraZeneca, for example, has a material patent cliff coming soon, but can its pipeline produce enough new drugs to offset the upcoming losses? As of July 2009, the company had 10 drugs either filed for review or in Phase III development and 29 in Phase II. The probabilities suggest it will be very difficult for the company to offset its patent cliff with its late-stage pipeline alone.

LEGISLATION AND REGULATION

Legislation can establish or change the rules of the game and how industries compete. State and federal agencies keep an eye on the industries and make sure they comply with rules and laws, which can have a material impact on a firm's operational and share price performance by making the environment relatively more or less difficult to operate in.

Legislation

The Health Care sector has what can be described as a love-hate relationship with the government. Legislation has the power to greatly impact the industry in a very positive or negative way. Unfortunately, legislation can be anticapitalistic and artificially create winners and losers. Legislation can also create a vast amount of uncertainty, which markets tend to hate.

For example, President Obama's 2009 priority was to reform health care, including lowering costs and expanding coverage to the uninsured. In late February, he delivered his budget proposal, which included reduced Medicare reimbursements, required increased outlays for Pharmaceuticals companies, and allowed bio-generic drugs. The uncertainty surrounding the proposal helped cause the Health Care sector to fall 5 percent the day it was released, with some Managed Care stocks declining as much as 20 percent.[5]

Debates intensified throughout the year as bills were introduced in House and Senate committees. Some of the topics and ideas discussed to address reform included establishing universal health care; increasing industry taxes; reducing government reimbursements; establishing a government-run health insurance plan to compete with the private industry; bio-pharma increasing drug rebates to the government; minimum loss ratios for insurance companies (the suggested loss ratio of 85 percent is generally higher than current industry levels); allowing for drug reimportation and generic biotech drugs; banning insurance companies from denying coverage based on pre-existing conditions; increasing fees on the insurance companies, medical equipment makers, and Pharmaceuticals companies; requiring employers to offer coverage and individuals to have coverage; and increasing funding for research. This laundry list is not exhaustive, but as you can see, any one of the measures mentioned could have a material impact on a firm's operations. Specifically, some feared creating a government-run insurance option would cause the demise of the private insurance industry. While some arguments could be part political grandstanding, it nevertheless causes uncertainty.

Regulation

Regulatory bodies can have a tremendous impact on a firm's success. For example, in the wake of the Vioxx debacle, the FDA and pharmaceutical manufacturers came under harsh criticism from the public and politicians. Politicians argued the FDA didn't do enough to monitor a drug's safety profile after it's approved for marketing. In response, the FDA tightened its standards, and many complain it resulted in drug approval delays and increased warning labels on existing drugs. Drug approval delays shorten the length of time a firm has patent exclusivity, while increased use of "black box" warnings can immediately impact sales.

Product Safety/Litigation

Product safety is a major concern for manufacturers, patients, regulators, and politicians. Sales of a product can materially fall after it's determined to have negative side effects. It can take years for a company to build its reputation, but it can be quickly wiped out with one unsafe product. Moreover, the media can sensationalize the problem, causing doctors, patients, and politicians to react before knowing all the facts. Safety problems can lead to lawsuits, which, if large enough, can financially cripple a firm.

Litigation and lawsuits, however, are a part of doing business in the Health Care sector. In extreme cases, lawsuits can bring a firm to its knees and cause investors to fear it will file for bankruptcy protection.

A good example is Merck's painkiller, Vioxx. The drug was FDA approved in 1999. In 2000, clinical trials to determine if Vioxx effectively treated rheumatoid arthritis suggested it may increase the risk of heart attack and stroke. The clinical results were disclosed to the FDA. However, for various reasons, management decided not to conduct a direct study to determine if Vioxx increased the risk of heart attacks. As time went on, more evidence highlighted the drug's risk profile. Finally, Merck voluntarily withdrew the drug from the market in 2004—a time when it was achieving over $2 billion in annual sales.

The Vioxx incident had several negative ramifications for Merck and the industry. First, it was a public relations nightmare—Vioxx was seen as the largest drug failure in history. Merck was also already dealing with patent expirations, and withdrawing one of its best-selling drugs had a material impact on sales and profits. Thousands of lawsuits were filed against Merck, which ultimately cost the company nearly $5 billion to settle.[6] The Vioxx issue resulted in a stricter regulatory environment, which had a real impact on the broader industry.

But in particular, Merck's stock was hammered when news about the drug withdrawal was released. Figure 6.1 illustrates Merck's share price during this period—it fell over 25 percent the day the news was announced and more than 40 percent over the next several weeks.[7] That big decline reflected the market's anticipation of negative ramifications.

Of course, no one could have predicted Merck's decision to remove Vioxx from the market or the sudden crash of its share price. Stock implosions can and do happen—which underscores the vital need for a well-diversified portfolio. As an analyst, you must determine

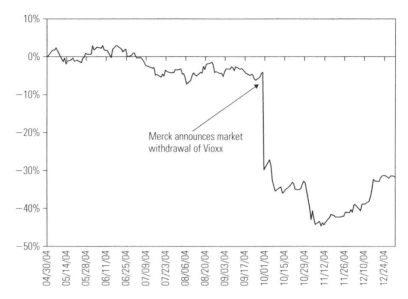

Figure 6.1   Merck Share Price Performance After the Vioxx Announcement

Source: Thomson Reuters.

if, after a stock crashes, the problems are insurmountable and the stock can't recover, or if the stock is being unfairly punished and might experience a big rebound. Knee-jerk reactions to a big stock price drop are rarely well-advised. Even in this chart you can see Merck did bounce back quite a lot after the big drop and more than double in price in the following few years as it redeemed itself by launching innovative new products like human papillomavirus (HPV) vaccine Gardasil and diabetes drug Januvia.

Black Box Warning

A black box warning is the strongest warning the FDA requires on a drug. It appears on the drug package and gets its name from the black border surrounding the warning information. A black box warning can have a negative impact on drug sales, and many argue the FDA increased the frequency of these labels as a result of pressure it received following the Vioxx debacle.

Here, you might want to consider how credible the lawsuits were, how likely the firm is to settle, and whether the firm has a pipeline that can help sustain it. Lawsuits can wreak near-term havoc—but you must determine whether the firm and/or industry will be impacted long-term.

RESPONDING TO CHALLENGES

So far, this chapter has outlined the challenges. But not all is doomed for the Health Care sector. These challenges are well known and have been with the sector to one degree or another since the advent of health care. Firms typically have established ways to deal with challenges, and better firms constantly innovate to find new ways to address their challenges, including:

- Pipeline development and tactical pricing
- Mergers and acquisitions
- Restructuring
- Lobbying

Pipeline Development and Tactical Pricing

Innovation and pipeline development are crucial to the Health Care industry. Firms continue to develop and invest in their pipelines, although many are more successful at it than others. In order to keep pipelines full to offset patent expirations, R&D budget growth typically remains relatively steady despite pressured sales.

Another way to develop a pipeline is engaging in joint ventures, co-developments, or licensing agreements with other companies. Licensing agreements link a firm that discovers a product with another that develops and/or sells it. The two firms then share the sales and profits. Co-development, joint ventures, and licensing agreements can be attractive options because they can lower the risk of development—but lower risk can mean lower return. For smaller firms, however, it can be a viable option because they may not have the needed manufacturing or distribution capabilities.

Firms can help offset revenue pressure from patent expirations and generic competition by raising prices on other drugs. This works particularly well when the drug is effective and has little competition. Price increases can be 10 percent or more, which can be substantial if the drug is widely prescribed.

Mergers and Acquisitions

Firms can acquire competitors to offset patent expirations, realize cost efficiencies, and grow operations. M&As are common in the Health Care industry, but larger scale M&A deals have recently increased as companies face the challenges detailed in this chapter. Not only are firms looking to acquire sales and pipelines in their own industry, but they may also look to expand into industries where they have little or no exposure. For example, a branded pharma firm may acquire a generic manufacturer, equipment maker, consumer products, or diagnostics equipment company to diversify its revenue stream.

On a macro scale, how do M&As impact a sector or the broader market? It depends on how deals are transacted. When one firm acquires another by paying cash (either with cash on hand or with borrowed funds), the acquired firm ceases to exist as an independent, publicly traded firm. Those shares are removed from the market, and sector share supply declines. Because stock prices are dictated by supply and demand, this should have a positive impact on prices if the demand for Health Care shares remains constant or rises. This bullish force becomes more powerful if the sector as a whole experiences a high level of cash-based mergers.

But mergers can also be transacted in stock. For example, Firm A is worth $20 billion and Firm B is worth $10 billion—$30 billion in total stock supply. Say Firm A wants to buy Firm B. Usually it will pay a premium, maybe 20 percent—and end up paying $12 billion. Firm A issues $12 billion in new Firm A stock, and Firm B ceases to exist. Except, where we once had $30 billion in total stock supply, we now have $32 billion. If this happens broadly, it can have a negative impact on prices if demand doesn't keep pace.

Deals can also be transacted partially in cash, partially in stock. For example, Firm A might pay a hybrid of $6 billion in cash, $6 billion in stock for Firm B. But most cash/stock deals tend to result in lower overall supply, which can be a bullish factor.

How do you know when cash-based deals or cash/stock hybrid deals are more likely to occur? Watch bond yields and earnings yields. A bond yield represents a firm's borrowing cost. The earnings yield is the reverse of the P/E ratio—the E/P (earnings per share over price per share). When earnings yields are higher than bond yields, a firm can borrow cheaply and buy a higher earnings yield—the difference between the higher earnings yield and the lower bond yield is profit. Done right, the deal finances itself and is immediately accretive to the acquirer's earnings. The acquirer's earnings per share rises, and, all else being equal, share price should follow. This is powerful incentive for CEOs to transact acquisitions (or buy back their own shares—the same concepts apply). Periods likely to see a higher rate of mergers and acquisitions are those when interest rates are generally benign and bond yields are lower than earnings yields—just as we saw in 2005, 2006, and 2007.

That's the sector-wide impact, but the effect on individual stocks can be subject to other considerations entirely, at least in the short term. In the very near term, sometimes Wall Street reacts favorably to deal news, sometimes negatively. As an investor, it's critical you don't get swayed by near-term knee-jerk reactions and understand how a deal impacts a firm for the longer term. For a deal to work, firms should find targets that fit well into their existing business or some-how introduce a new, competitive value proposition.

Restructuring

Restructuring operations and improving efficiency is another method of combating slowing growth. Generally, a firm will restructure when management believes its operations are not appropriately aligned with the current environment. Frequently, corporate restructuring takes place when a company's operating outlook is challenging, but it can also happen in firms preparing for a high-growth environment.

A company can restructure one or several departments. "Improving efficiency" can be a euphemism for laying people off, but the operating environment may warrant such a move. Or certain departments, such as R&D, may not be very productive, requiring a reassessment in order to simplify or outsource operations. The sales force may need to be reduced because the selling environment has changed. For example, because of the growing importance for drug firms to have their drugs on the formulary list and increased sales to the government and insurance firms, sales strategies and tactics have had to evolve.

Firms may also restructure their supply chains to lower costs. Restructuring may also lead firms to divest certain businesses or acquire firms to gain access to missing expertise. Restructuring, however, is usually a temporary solution. Without any catalyst to reignite sales, it may only slow bottom-line bleeding. But if coupled with increasing sales, restructuring can add a significant earnings boost.

Lobbying

Since the government is heavily involved in health care, it's imperative the Health Care industry be involved to help shape and guide reform measures. After all, no one knows the Health Care industry better than its participants—and the industry employs one of the most powerful lobbying groups. The health care lobby employs 3,000 registered lobbyists, which equates to six lobbyists for each member of Congress.[8] Additionally, many lobbyists are former politicians. Effective lobbying can result in a relatively more favorable outcome for the industry. Relative is the key word because when it comes to investing, the outcome relative to expectations is what drives share price performance.

Case Study: Pfizer While nearly all Health Care firms experience challenges and have myriad ways to respond to them, we'll take a closer look at one firm—Pfizer—and how it has dealt with some common challenges.

Pfizer's stock price fell from $48 in mid-June of 2000 to $12 in March 2009. Two bear markets (2000–2002 and 2007–2009) likely contributed to its falling price, but the share price fell even during much of the 2003 to 2007 five-year bull market. Fundamental reasons such as a weak pipeline, patent expirations, and sales pressure likely helped drive price declines.

Patent Expirations and Pricing Pressures Pfizer has a looming patent cliff starting in 2010 and extending through 2015—it will lose patent protection for Xalatan (eye pressure), Viagra (erectile dysfunction), Detrol (overactive bladder), Geodon (schizophrenia/bipolar), Celebrex (arthritis), and Caduet (blood pressure/cholesterol). Moreover, in 2011, the patent for Lipitor (cholesterol) will expire. (Lipitor accounted for approximately 26 percent of Pfizer's 2008 total revenues.[9]) Combined with Lipitor, these drugs represented 44 percent of 2008 sales.[10] Sales of Lipitor are already being pressured by generic competition—sales peaked at $12.9 billion in 2006, but have since declined $500 million annually to approximately $12.4 billion as of 2008.[11]

Weak Pipeline In 2006, Pfizer's key pipeline drug, torcetrapib, was expected to replace Lipitor—there were high expectations for this drug. Torcetrapib was supposed to raise the high-density lipoproteins (HDL, the "healthy" cholesterol) and lower the low-density lipoproteins (LDL, the "unhealthy" cholesterol—think of it as H for healthy and L for lousy) in the blood. Pfizer spent approximately $1 billion developing the drug, but in December 2006, it announced torcetrapib failed in Phase III development. The firm's pipeline looked weak in 2006, and it seemed Pfizer might not have the capacity to offset upcoming patent expirations and grow revenues.

Responding to Challenges—Restructuring Soon after the torce-trapib failure, the company announced a restructuring plan to focus on developing its biotech products and saving $2 billion per year by laying off 10,000 employees, selling off nearly one-half of its manufacturing plants, and reorganizing and consolidating R&D efforts. This restructuring effort was preceded by the firm's decision to sell its consumer division to Johnson & Johnson in June 2006 for $16 billion—Pfizer claimed it wanted to focus on its drug business.

R&D Investments Pfizer continues to invest over $7 billion per year in its pipeline, and it has had some success launching Lyrica (fibromyalgia), Sutent (cancer), and the antismoking drug Chantix. The latter two were expected to be blockbusters, but soon, patients taking Chantix began developing negative psychological side effects such as aggression, depression, and suicidal thoughts. A black box warning was placed on Chantix, and sales declined.

M&A Restructuring operations may make a firm more efficient, but a company can't cost-cut its way out of the problems of patent expirations and a weak pipeline. That's why, in January 2009, Pfizer announced the $68 billion acquisition of Wyeth—Pfizer believed the merger would save approximately $4 billion in operational costs. By acquiring Wyeth, Pfizer gained pipeline drugs, and Wyeth's annual sales of $20 billion roughly equated to the expected dollar amount of Pfizer's lost sales due to patent expiration between 2010 and 2015. The acquisition should help Pfizer diversify its revenue stream, lessen the patent-cliff impact, and achieve efficiency gains.

But while the Wyeth acquisition was large and should provide some benefits, it won't necessarily increase shareholder value—in fact, studies have shown many large-scale M&A deals fail to increase shareholder value. Only time will tell if Pfizer can make this deal a profitable one.

Chapter Recap

- Health Care has traditionally been known as a growth industry as demand, innovation, and pricing power led the sector to grow faster than the general economy.
- Recently, however, many companies, particularly in the Pharmaceuticals industry (which dominates the sector), are beginning to take on value characteristics as the sector addresses the challenges of patent expirations, competition, a tight regulatory environment, a dearth of pipeline products, politics, pricing pressures, and litigation.
- Companies are addressing the sector's challenges by developing their pipelines, engaging in M&A and licensing agreements, increasing prices on unique drugs with little competition, restructuring, and lobbying Congress.
- Understanding these challenges and how effectively a company responds to its challenges is vital to your analysis of Health Care stocks.

III

THINKING LIKE A
PORTFOLIO MANAGER

7

THE TOP-DOWN METHOD

So if you're bullish on Health Care, how much of your portfolio should you put in Health Care stocks? Twenty-five percent? Fifty? One hundred percent? This question concerns portfolio management. Most investors concern themselves only with individual companies ("I like Johnson & Johnson, so I'll buy some") without considering how they fit into their overall portfolio. But this is no way to manage your money.

In this part of the book, we show you how to analyze Health Care companies like a top-down portfolio manager. This includes a full description of the top-down method, how to use benchmarks, and how the top-down method applies to the Health Care sector. We then explore security analysis in Chapter 8, where we provide a framework for analyzing any company and discuss many of the important questions to ask when analyzing Health Care companies. Finally, in Chapter 9, we conclude by giving a few examples of specific investing strategies for the Health Care sector.

INVESTING IS A SCIENCE

Too many investors today think investing has "rules"—that all one must do to succeed in investing for the long run is find the right set of investing rules. But that simply doesn't work. Why? All well-known and widely discussed information is already reflected in stock prices. This is a basic tenet of market theory and commonly referred to as "market efficiency." So if you see a headline about a stock you follow, there's no use trading on that information—it's already priced in. You missed the move.

If everything known is already discounted in prices, the only way to consistently beat the market is to know something others don't. Think about it: There are many intelligent investors and longtime professionals who fail to beat the market year after year, most with the same access to information as anyone else, if not more. Why?

Because most view investing as a craft. They think, "If I learn the craft of value investing and all its rules, then I can be a successful investor using that method." But that simply can't work because by definition, all the conventional ways of thinking about value investing will already be widely known and thus priced in. In fact, most investment styles are very well-known and already widely practiced. There are undoubtedly millions of investors out there much like you, looking at the same metrics and information you are. So there isn't much power in them. Even the investing techniques themselves are widely known—taught to millions in universities and practiced by hundreds of thousands of professionals globally. There's no edge.

Moreover, it's been demonstrated investment styles move in and out of favor over time—no one style or category is inherently better than another in the long run. You may think "value" investing works wonders to beat markets, but the fact is growth stocks will trounce value at times.

The key to beating stock markets lies in being dynamic—never adhering for all time to a single investment idea—and gleaning information the market hasn't yet priced in. In other words, you cannot adhere to a single set of "rules" and hope to outperform markets over time.

So how can you beat the markets? By thinking of investing as a science.

Einstein's Brain and the Stock Market

If he weren't so busy becoming the most renowned scientist of the twentieth century, Albert Einstein would have made a killing on Wall Street—but not because he had such a high IQ. Granted, he was immensely intelligent, but a high IQ alone does not make a market guru. (If it did, MIT professors would be making millions managing money instead of teaching.) Instead, it's the style of his thought and the method of his work that matter.

In the little we know about Einstein's investment track record, he didn't do very well. He lost most of his Nobel Prize money in bad bond ventures.[1] Heck, Sir Isaac Newton may have given us the three laws of motion, but even his talents didn't extend to investing. He lost his shirt in the South Sea Bubble of the early 1700s, explaining later, "I can calculate the movement of the stars, but not the madness of men."

So why believe Einstein would have been a great portfolio manager if he had put his mind to it? In short, Einstein was a true and highly creative scientist. He didn't take the acknowledged rules of physics as such—he used prior knowledge, logic, and creativity combined with the rigors of verifiable, testable scientific methods to create an entirely new view of the cosmos. In other words, he was dynamic and gleaned knowledge others didn't have. Investors should do the same. (Not to worry, you won't need advanced calculus to do it.)

Einstein's unique character gave him an edge—he truly had a mind made to beat markets. Scientists have studied his work, his speeches, his letters, even his brain (literally) to find the secret of his intellect. In all, his approach to information processing and idea generation, his willingness to go against the grain of the establishment, and his relentless pursuit of answers to questions no one else was asking ultimately made him a genius.

Both his contemporaries and most biographers agree one of Einstein's foremost gifts was his ability to discern "the big picture." Unlike many scientists who could easily drown themselves in data minutiae, Einstein had an ability to see above the fray. Another way to say this is he could take the same information everyone else at his time was looking at and interpret it differently, yet correctly. He accomplished this using his talent for extracting the most important data from what he studied and linking them together in innovative ways no one else could.

Einstein called this "combinatory play." Similar to a child experimenting with a new Lego set, Einstein would combine and recombine seemingly unrelated ideas, concepts, and images to produce new, original discoveries. In the end, almost all new ideas are merely the combination of existing ones in one form or another. Take $E = mc^2$: Einstein was not the first to discover the concepts of energy, mass, or the speed of light; rather, he combined these concepts in a novel way, and in the process, altered how we view the universe.[2]

Einstein's combinatory play is a terrific metaphor for stock investing. To be a successful market strategist, you must be able to extract the most important data from all of the "noise" permeating today's markets and generate conclusions the market hasn't yet appreciated. Central to this task is your ability to link data together in unique ways and produce new insights and themes for your portfolio in the process.

Einstein learned science basics just like his peers. But once he had those mastered, he directed his brain to challenging prior assumptions and inventing entirely different lenses to look through.

This is why this book isn't intended to give you a "silver bullet" for picking the right Health Care stocks. The fact is, the "right" Health Care stocks will be different in different times and situations. You don't have to be Einstein, you just should think differently—and like a scientist—if you want to beat markets.

THE TOP-DOWN METHOD

Overwhelmingly, investment professionals today do what can broadly be labeled "bottom-up" investing. Their emphasis is on stock selection. A typical bottom-up investor researches an assortment of companies and attempts to pick those with the greatest likelihood of outperforming the market based on individual merits. The selected securities are cobbled together to form a portfolio, and factors like country and economic sector exposure are purely residuals of security selection, not planned decisions.

"Top-down" investing reverses the order. A top-down investor first analyzes big picture factors like economics, politics, and sentiment to forecast which investment categories are most likely to outperform the market. Only then does a top-down investor begin looking at individual securities. Top-down investing is inevitably more concerned with a portfolio's aggregate exposure to investment categories than with any individual security. Thus, top-down is an inherently *dynamic* mode of investing because investment strategies are based upon the prevailing market and economic environment (which changes often).

There's significant debate in the investment community as to which approach is superior. This book's goal is not to reject bottom-up investing—there are indeed investors who've successfully utilized bottom-up approaches. Rather, the goal is to introduce a comprehensive and flexible methodology that any investor could use to build a portfolio designed to beat the global stock market in any investment environment. It's a framework for gleaning new insights and making good on information not already reflected in stock prices.

Before we describe the method, let's explore several key reasons why a top-down approach is advantageous:

- **Scalability.** A bottom-up process is akin to looking for needles in a haystack. A top-down process is akin to seeking the haystacks with the highest concentrations of needles. Globally, there are nearly 25,000 publicly traded stocks. Even the largest institutions with the greatest research resources cannot hope to adequately examine all these companies. Smaller institutions and individual investors must prioritize where to focus their limited resources. Unlike a bottom-up process, a top-down process makes this gargantuan task manageable by determining, upfront, what slices of the market to examine at the security level.
- **Enhanced stock selection.** Well-designed top-down processes generate insights that can greatly enhance stock selection.

Macroeconomic or political analysis, for instance, can help determine what types of strategic attributes will face head or tailwinds (see Chapter 8 for a full explanation).

- **Risk control.** Bottom-up processes are highly subject to unintended risk concentrations. Top-down processes are inherently better suited to manage risk exposures throughout the investment process.
- **Macro overview.** Top-down processes are more conducive to avoiding macro-driven calamities like the bursting of the Japan bubble in the 1990s, the Technology bubble in 2000, or the bear markets of 2000 to 2002 and 2007 to 2009. No matter how good an individual company may be, it is still beholden to sector, regional, and broad market factors. In fact, there is evidence macro factors can largely determine a stock's performance regardless of individual merit.

Top-Down Means Thinking 70-20-10

A top-down investment process also helps focus on what's most important to investment results: asset allocation and sub-asset allocation decisions. Many investors focus most of their attention on security-level portfolio decisions, like picking individual stocks they think will perform well. However, studies have shown that over 90 percent of return variability is derived from asset allocation decisions, not market timing or stock selection.[3]

Our research shows about 70 percent of return variability is derived from asset allocation, 20 percent from sub-asset allocation (such as country, sector, size, and style), and 10 percent from security selection. While security selection can make a significant difference over time, higher-level portfolio decisions dominate investment results more often than not.

The balance of this chapter defines the various steps in the top-down method, specifically as they relate to making country, sector, and style decisions. This same basic framework can be applied to portfolios to make allocations within sectors. At the end of the chapter, we detail how this framework can be applied to the Health Care sector.

Benchmarks

A key part of the top-down model is using benchmarks. A benchmark is typically a broad-based index of securities such as the S&P 500, MSCI World, or Russell 2000. Benchmarks are indispensible road maps for structuring a portfolio, monitoring risk, and judging performance over time.

Tactically, a portfolio should be structured to maximize the probability of consistently beating the benchmark. This is inherently different than maximizing returns. Unlike aiming to achieve some fixed rate of return each year, which will cause disappointment relative to peers when capital markets are very strong and is potentially unrealistic when the capital markets are very weak, a properly benchmarked portfolio provides a realistic guide for dealing with uncertain market conditions.

Portfolio construction begins by evaluating the characteristics of the chosen benchmark: sector weights, country weights, and market cap and valuations. Then an expected risk and return is assigned to each of these segments (based on portfolio drivers), and the most attractive areas are overweighted, while the least attractive are underweighted. Table 7.1 shows MSCI World benchmark sector characteristics

Table 7.1   MSCI World Characteristics: Sectors

Sector	Weight
Financials	21.0%
Information Technology	12.2%
Industrials	11.1%
Energy	10.7%
Consumer Discretionary	10.0%
Consumer Staples	9.9%
Health Care	9.5%
Materials	7.3%
Utilities	4.2%
Telecommunication Services	4.0%

Source: Thomson Reuters; MSCI, Inc.[4] as of 12/31/09.

Table 7.2   MSCI World Characteristics: Countries

Country	Weight
US	49.9%
Japan	10.2%
UK	9.5%
Canada	5.1%
France	4.6%
Australia	4.0%
Germany	3.5%
Switzerland	3.4%
Spain	1.7%
Italy	1.4%
Sweden	1.3%
Netherlands	1.2%
Hong Kong	1.1%
Singapore	0.7%
Finland	0.5%
Denmark	0.5%
Belgium	0.4%
Norway	0.3%
Greece	0.2%
Austria	0.2%
Ireland	0.1%
Portugal	0.1%
New Zealand	0.0%

Source: Thomson Reuters; MSCI, Inc.[5] as of 12/31/09.

as of December 31, 2009, as an example, while Table 7.2 shows country characteristics, and Table 7.3 shows market cap and valuations.

Based on benchmark characteristics, portfolio drivers are then used to determine country, sector, and style decisions for the portfolio. For example, in Table 7.1, the Financials sector weight of the MSCI World Index is 21 percent. Therefore, a portfolio managed against this benchmark would consider a 21 percent weight in

Table 7.3   MSCI World Characteristics: Market Cap and
Valuations

Name	Valuations
Median Market Cap	$6.8 billion
Weighted Average Market Cap	$63.3 billion
P/E	15.9
P/B	2.0
Div Yield	2.4
P/CF	10.4
P/S	2.1
Number of Holdings	1,656

Notes: P/E = price-earnings ratio; P/B = price-to-book ratio; Div Yield = dividend yield; P/CF = price-to-cash-flow ratio; P/S = price-to-sales ratio.
Source: Thomson Reuters as of 12/31/09.

Financials "neutral," or market-weighted. If you believe Financials will perform better than the market in the foreseeable future, then you would "overweight" the sector, or hold more than 21 percent of your portfolio in Financials stocks. The reverse is true for an "underweight"— you'd hold less than 21 percent in Financials if you were pessimistic on the sector looking ahead.

Note that being pessimistic on Financials *doesn't necessarily mean holding zero financial stocks.* It might only mean holding a lesser percentage of stocks in your portfolio than the benchmark. This is an important feature of benchmarking—it allows an investor to make strategic decisions on sectors and countries while maintaining diversification, thus managing risk more appropriately.

For the Health Care sector, we can use Health Care-specific benchmarks like the S&P 500 Health Care, MSCI World Health Care, or Russell 2000 Health Care indexes. The components of these benchmarks can then be evaluated at a more detailed level such as industry and sub-industry weights. (For example, we broke out MSCI World industry and sub-industry benchmark weights in Chapter 4.)

TOP-DOWN DECONSTRUCTED

The top-down method begins by first analyzing the macro environment. It asks the "big" questions like: Do you think stocks will go up or down in the next 12 months? If so, which countries or sectors should benefit most? Once you have decided on these high-level portfolio "drivers" (sometimes called "themes"), you can examine various macro portfolio drivers to make general overweight and underweight decisions for countries, sectors, industries, and sub-industries versus your benchmark.

For instance, let's say we've determined a macroeconomic driver that goes something like this: "In the next 12 months, I believe global government health care spending will be greater than most expect." That's a very high-level statement with important implications for your portfolio. It means you'd want to search for industries, and ultimately stocks, that would benefit most from increased government health care spending.

The second step in top-down is applying quantitative screening criteria to narrow the choice set of stocks. Since, in our hypothetical example, we believe government health care spending will be higher than many expect, perhaps we could be bullish on Health Care Providers & Services stocks. But which ones? Are you bullish on, say, Managed Care? Services? Facilities? Do you want exposure to the US or another region? Do you want small cap Health Care companies or large cap? And what about valuations? Are you looking for growth or value? (Size and growth/value categories are often referred to as "style" decisions.) These criteria and more can help you narrow the list of stocks you might buy.

The third and final step is performing fundamental analysis on individual stocks. Notice that a great deal of thinking, analysis, and work is done before you ever think about individual stocks. That's the key to the top-down approach: It emphasizes high-level themes and funnels its way down to individual stocks, as is illustrated in Figure 7.1.

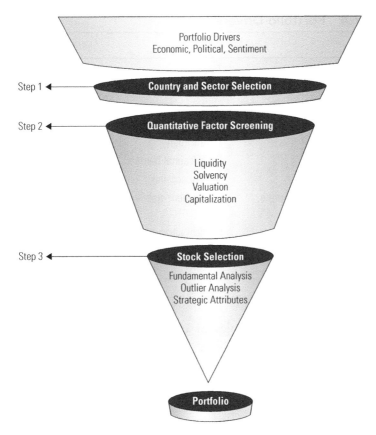

Figure 7.1   Top-Down Deconstructed

Step 1: Analyze Portfolio Drivers and Country and Sector Selection

Let's examine the first step in the top-down method more closely. In order to make top-down decisions, we develop and analyze what we call *portfolio drivers* (as mentioned previously). We segment these portfolio drivers in three general categories: *economic, political,* and *sentiment.*

Portfolio drivers are what drive the performance of a broad category of stocks. Accurately identifying current and future drivers will help you find areas of the market most likely to outperform or underperform your benchmark (i.e., the broader stock market).

Table 7.4   Portfolio Drivers

Economic	Political	Sentiment
Yield curve spread	Taxation	Mutual fund flows
Relative GDP growth	Property rights	Relative style and asset class valuations
Monetary base/growth	Structural reform	Media coverage
Currency strength	Privatization	Institutional searches
Relative interest rates	Trade/capital barriers	Consumer confidence
Inflation	Current account	Foreign investment
Debt level (sovereign, corporate, consumer)	Government stability	Professional investor forecasts
Infrastructure spending	Political turnover	Momentum cycle analysis
M&A, issuance, and repurchase activity	Wars/conflicts	Risk aversion

Table 7.4 shows examples of each type of portfolio driver. It's important to note these drivers are by no means comprehensive, nor are they valid for all time periods. In fact, correctly identifying new portfolio drivers is essential to beating the market in the long term.

Economic Drivers Economic drivers are anything related to the macroeconomic environment. This could include monetary policy, interest rates, lending activity, yield curve analysis, relative GDP growth analysis, and a myriad of others. What economic forces are likely to drive GDP growth throughout countries in the world? What is the outlook for interest rates, and how would that impact sectors? What is the outlook for technology and infrastructure spending among countries?

Economic drivers pertain not only to the fundamental outlook of the economy (GDP growth, interest rates, inflation), but also to the stock market (valuations, M&A activity, share buybacks). As an investor, it's your job to identify these drivers and determine how they'll impact your overall portfolio and each of its segments.

The following is a list of economic drivers that could impact portfolio performance:

- US economic growth will be higher than consensus expectations.
- European Union interest rates will remain benign.
- Mergers, acquisitions, and share buybacks will be strong.
- Emerging markets growth will drive commodity demand.

Political Drivers Political drivers can be country-specific, pertain to regions (EU, for example) or affect interaction between countries or regions (such as trade policies). These drivers are more concerned with categories such as taxation, government stability, fiscal policy, and political turnover. Which countries are experiencing a change in government that could have a meaningful impact on their economies? Which sectors could be at risk from new taxation or legislation? Which countries are undergoing pro-growth reforms?

Political drivers will help determine the relative attractiveness of market segments and countries based on the outlook for the political environment. Be warned, however: Most investors suffer from "home country bias," where they ascribe too much emphasis to the politics of their own country. Always keep in mind it's a big, interconnected world out there, and geopolitical developments everywhere can have implications.

What are possible political drivers you can find? The following is a list of examples that can drive stocks up or down.

- Political party change in Japan driving pro-growth reforms
- New tax policies in Germany stalling economic growth
- Protests, government coups, conflict driving political instability in Thailand

Sentiment Drivers Sentiment drivers attempt to measure consensus thinking about investment categories. Ideally, drivers identify market opportunities where sentiment is different from reality. For example, let's say you observe current broad market sentiment expects a US recession in the next year. But you disagree and believe GDP growth will be strong. This presents an excellent opportunity for excess returns. You can load up on stocks that will benefit from an economic boom and watch the prices rise as the rest of the market realizes it much later.

Since the market is a discounter of all known information, it's important to try and identify what the market is pricing in. The interpretation of such investor drivers is typically counterintuitive (avoid what is overly popular and seek what is largely unpopular). Looking forward, which sectors are investors most bullish about and why? What countries or sectors are widely discussed in the media? What market segments have been bid up recently based on something other than fundamentals? If the market's perception is different from fundamentals in the short term, stocks will eventually correct themselves to reflect reality in the long term.

A note of caution: Gauging market sentiment does not mean being a *contrarian*. Contrarians are investors who simply do the

How to Create Your Own Investment Drivers

In order to form your own investment drivers, the first step is accessing a wide array of data from multiple sources. For country drivers, this could range from globally focused publications like the *Wall Street Journal* or *Financial Times* to regional newspapers or government data. For sector drivers, this could include reading trade publications or following major company announcements.

Remember, however, that markets are efficient—they reflect all widely known information. Most pertinent information about public companies is, well, *public*. Which means the market already knows. News travels fast, and investors with the knowledge and expectations are absorbed by markets very quickly. Those seeking to profit on a bit of news, rumor, or speculation must acknowledge the market will probably move faster than they can. Therefore, in order to consistently generate excess returns, you must either know something others don't or interpret widely known information differently and correctly from the crowd. (For a detailed discussion on these factors and more, read *The Only Three Questions That Count* by Ken Fisher.)

opposite of what most believe will happen. Instead, find places where sentiment (people's beliefs) doesn't match what you believe is reality and over- or underweight sections of your portfolio accordingly, relative to your benchmark. Examples of sentiment drivers include:

- Investors remain pessimistic about Technology despite improving fundamentals.
- Sentiment for the Chinese stock market approaching euphoria, stretching valuations.
- Professional investors universally forecast US small cap stocks to outperform.

Step 2: Quantitative Factor Screening

Step two in the top-down method is screening for quantitative factors. This allows you to narrow the potential list of stocks once your portfolio drivers are in place.

There are thousands and thousands of stocks out there, so it's vital to use a series of factors like market capitalization and valuations to narrow the field a bit. Securities passing this screen are then subjected to further quantitative analysis that eliminates companies with excessive risk profiles relative to their peer group, such as companies with excessive leverage or balance sheet risk and securities lacking sufficient liquidity for investment.

The rigidity of the quantitative screens is entirely up to you, and will determine the number of companies on your prospect list. The more rigid the criteria, the fewer the companies that make the list. Broader criteria will increase the number of companies.

Examples   How can you perform such a screen? Here are two examples of quantitative factor screenings to show how broad or specific you can be. You might want to apply very strict criteria, or you may prefer to be broader.

Strict Criteria

- First, you decide you want to search for only Health Care firms. By definition, that excludes all companies from the other nine sectors. Already, you've narrowed the field a lot!
- Now, let's say that based on your high-level drivers, you only want European Health Care stocks. By excluding all other regions besides Europe, you've narrowed the field even more.
- Next, let's decide to search only for Equipment firms in the Health Care sector.
- Perhaps you don't believe very small stocks are preferable, so you limit market capitalization to $3 billion and above.
- Last, let's set some parameters for valuation:
  - P/E (price-to-earnings) less than 2×
  - P/B (price-to-book) less than 2×
  - P/CF (price-to-cash-flow) less than 10×
  - P/S (price-to-sales) less than 3×

This rigorous process of selecting parameters will yield a small number of stocks to research, all based on your higher-level themes. But maybe you have reason to be less specific and want to do a broader screen because you think Health Care in general is a good place to be.

Broad Criteria

- Health Care sector
- Global (no country or region restrictions)
- Market caps above $1 billion

This selection process is much broader and obviously gives you a much longer list of stocks to choose from. Neither a strict or broad screen is inherently better than the other. It just depends on how well-formed and specific your higher-level themes are. Obviously, a stricter screen means less work for you in step three—actual stock selection.

Step 3: Stock Selection

After narrowing the prospect list, your final step is identifying individual securities possessing strategic attributes consistent with higher-level portfolio themes. (We'll cover the stock selection process specifically in more detail in Chapter 8.) Your stock selection process should attempt to accomplish two goals:

1. Find firms possessing strategic attributes consistent with higher-level portfolio themes, derived from the drivers that give those firms a competitive advantage versus their peers. For example, if you believe owning firms with dominant market shares in consolidating industries is a favorable characteristic, you would search for firms with that profile.

2. Maximize the likelihood of beating the category of stocks you are analyzing. For example, if you want a certain portfolio weight of Biotechnology companies and need 4 stocks out of 12 meeting the quantitative criteria, you then pick the 4 that, as a group, maximize the likelihood of beating all 12 as a whole. This is different than trying to pick "the best four." By avoiding stocks likely to be extreme or "weird" outliers versus the group, you can reduce portfolio risk while adding value at the security selection level.

In lieu of picking individual securities, there are other ways to exploit high-level themes in the top-down process. For instance, if you feel strongly about a particular sub-industry but don't think you can add value through individual security analysis, it may be more prudent to buy a group of companies in the sub-industry or a category product like an exchange-traded fund (ETF). There is a growing variety of ETFs that track the domestic and global Health Care sector, industries, and even specific commodity prices. This way, you can be sure to gain broad Health Care exposure without much stock-specific risk. (For more information on ETFs, visit www.ishares.com, www.sectorspdr.com, or www.masterdata.com.)

MANAGING AGAINST A HEALTH CARE BENCHMARK

Now we can practice translating this specifically to your Health Care allocation. Just as you analyze the components of your benchmark to determine country and sector components in a top-down strategy,

Table 7.5   MSCI World Health Care Sub-Industry Weights Versus Sample Portfolio

Sub-Industry	MSCI World Health Care	Sample Portfolio
Pharmaceuticals	61%	?
Health Care Equipment	14%	?
Biotechnology	9%	?
Health Care Services	5%	?
Managed Health Care	4%	?
Life Sciences Tools & Services	3%	?
Health Care Distributors	3%	?
Health Care Supplies	1%	?
Health Care Technology	0%	?
Health Care Facilities	0%	?
Total	100%	100%

Source: Thomson Reuters; MSCI, Inc.[6] as of 12/31/09.

you must analyze each sector's components, as we did in Chapter 4. To demonstrate how, we'll use the MSCI World Health Care Sector index as the benchmark. Table 7.5 shows the MSCI World Health Care sub-industry weights as of December 31, 2009. We don't know what the sample portfolio weights should be, but we know it should add up to 100 percent. Of course, if managing against a broader benchmark, your Health Care sector weight may add up to more or less than the Health Care weight in the benchmark, depending on over- or underweight decisions.

Keeping the sub-industry weights in mind will help mitigate benchmark risk. If you have a portfolio of stocks with the same sub-industry weights as the MSCI World Health Care Index, you're *neutral*—taking no benchmark risk. However, if you feel strongly about a sub-industry, like Health Care Distributors, and decide to only purchase those firms (one of the smallest weights in the sector), you're taking a huge benchmark risk. The same is true if you significantly *underweight* a sub-industry. All the same rules apply when you do this from a broader portfolio perspective, as we did earlier in this chapter.

The benchmark's sub-industry weights provide a jumping-off point for making further portfolio decisions. Once you make higher-level

Table 7.6   Portfolio A

Sub-Industry	MSCI World Health Care	Sample Portfolio	Difference
Pharmaceuticals	61%	55%	−6%
Health Care Equipment	14%	20%	6%
Biotechnology	9%	7%	−2%
Health Care Services	5%	6%	1%
Managed Health Care	4%	6%	2%
Life Sciences Tools & Services	3%	6%	3%
Health Care Distributors	3%	0%	−3%
Health Care Supplies	1%	0%	−1%
Health Care Technology	0%	0%	0%
Health Care Facilities	0%	0%	0%
Total	100%	100%	0%

Source: Thomson Reuters; MSCI, Inc.[7] as of 12/31/09.

decisions on the sub-industries, you can make choices versus the benchmark by overweighting the sub-industries you feel likeliest to perform best and underweighting those likeliest to perform worst. Table 7.6 shows how you can make different portfolio bets against the benchmark by over- and underweighting sub-industries.

Note: Portfolio A might be a portfolio of all Health Care stocks, or it can simply represent a neutral Health Care sector allocation in a larger portfolio.

The "Difference" column shows the relative difference between the benchmark and Portfolio A. In this example, Portfolio A is most overweight to Health Care Equipment and most underweight to Pharmaceuticals.

In other words, for this hypothetical example, Portfolio A's owner expects Health Care Equipment, Services, Managed Care, and Life Sciences to outperform the sector and Pharmaceuticals, Biotechnology, Distributors, and Supplies to underperform the sector. But in terms of benchmark risk, Portfolio A remains fairly close to the benchmark weights, so its relative risk is quite modest. This is extremely important: By managing against a benchmark, you can make strategic choices to beat the index and are well-diversified within the sector without concentrating too heavily in a specific area.

Table 7.7   Portfolio B

Sub-Industry	MSCI World Health Care	Sample Portfolio	Difference
Pharmaceuticals	61%	0%	−61%
Health Care Equipment	14%	0%	−14%
Biotechnology	9%	0%	−9%
Health Care Services	5%	0%	−5%
Managed Health Care	4%	100%	96%
Life Sciences Tools & Services	3%	0%	−3%
Health Care Distributors	3%	0%	−3%
Health Care Supplies	1%	0%	−1%
Health Care Technology	0%	0%	0%
Health Care Facilities	0%	0%	0%
Total	100%	100%	0%

Source: Thomson Reuters; MSCI, Inc.[8] as of 12/31/09.

Table 7.7 is another example of relative portfolio weighting versus the benchmark. Portfolio B is significantly underweight to Pharmaceuticals, with exposure only to Managed Health Care. Because the sub-industry weights are so different from the benchmark, Portfolio B takes on substantially more relative risk than Portfolio A.

Regardless of how your portfolio is positioned relative to the benchmark, it's important to use benchmarks to identify where your relative risks are before investing. Knowing the benchmark weights and having opinions on the future performance of each sub-industry is a crucial step in building a portfolio designed to beat the benchmark. Should you make the correct overweight and underweight decisions, you're likelier to beat the benchmark regardless of the individual securities held within. But even if you're wrong, you'll have diversified enough not to lose your shirt.

Chapter Recap

A more effective approach to sector analysis is "top-down." A top-down investment methodology analyzes big-picture factors such as economics, politics, and sentiment to forecast which investment categories are likely to outperform the market. A key part of the process is the use of benchmarks (such as the MSCI World Health Care or S&P 500 Health Care indexes), which are used as guidelines for building portfolios, monitoring performance, and managing risk. By analyzing portfolio drivers, we can identify which Health Care industries and sub-industries are most attractive and unattractive, ultimately filtering down to stock selection.

- The top-down investment methodology first identifies and analyzes high-level portfolio drivers affecting broad categories of stocks. These drivers help determine portfolio country, sector, and style weights. The same methodology can be applied to a specific sector to determine industry and sub-industry weights.
- Quantitative factor screening helps narrow the list of potential portfolio holdings based on characteristics such as valuations, liquidity, and solvency.
- Stock selection is the last step in the top-down process. Stock selection attempts to find companies possessing strategic attributes consistent with higher-level portfolio drivers.
- Stock selection also attempts to find companies with the greatest probability of outperforming their peers.
- It's helpful to use a Health Care benchmark as a guide when constructing a portfolio to determine your sub-industry overweights and underweights.

8

SECURITY ANALYSIS

Now that we've covered the top-down method, let's pick some stocks. This chapter walks you through analyzing individual Health Care firms using the top-down method presented in Chapter 7. Specifically, we'll demonstrate a five-step process for analyzing firms relative to peers.

Every firm and every stock is different, and viewing them through the right lens is vital. Investors need a functional, consistent, and reusable framework for analyzing securities across the sector. While by no means comprehensive, the framework provided and the questions at this chapter's end should serve as good starting points to help identify strategic attributes and company-specific risks.

While volumes have been written about individual security analysis, a top-down investment approach de-emphasizes the importance of stock selection in a portfolio. As such, we'll talk about the basics of stock analysis for the beginner to intermediate investor. For a more thorough understanding of financial statement analysis, valuations, modeling, and other tools of security analysis, additional reading is suggested.

Top-Down Recap

As covered in Chapter 7, you can use the top-down method to make your biggest, most important portfolio decisions first. However, the same process applies when picking stocks, and those high-level portfolio decisions ultimately filter down to individual securities.

Step one is analyzing the broader global economy and identifying various macro drivers affecting entire sectors or industries. Using the drivers, you can make general allocation decisions for countries, sectors, industries, and sub-industries versus the given benchmark. Step two is applying quantitative screening criteria to narrow the choice set of stocks. It's not until all those decisions are made that we get to analyze individual stocks. Security analysis is the third and final step.

For the rest of the chapter, we assume you have already established a benchmark, solidified portfolio themes, made sub-industry overweight and underweight decisions, and are ready to analyze firms within a peer group. (A peer group is a group of stocks you'd generally expect to perform similarly because they operate in the same industry, possibly share the same geography, and have similar quantitative attributes.)

MAKE YOUR SELECTION

Security analysis is nowhere near as complicated as it may seem—but that doesn't mean it's easy. Similar to your goal in choosing industry and sector weights, you've got one basic task: spot opportunities not currently discounted into prices. Or, put differently, know something others don't. Investors should analyze firms by taking consensus expectations for a company's estimated financial results and then assessing whether it will perform below, in line with, or above those baseline expectations. Profit opportunities arise when your expectations are different and more accurate than consensus expectations. Trading on widely known information or consensus expectations adds no value to the stock selection process. Doing so is really no different than trading on a coin flip.

The top-down method offers two ways to spot such opportunities. First, accurately predict high-level, macro themes affecting an industry or group of companies—these are your portfolio drivers. Second, find firms that will benefit most if those high-level themes and drivers play out. This is done by finding firms with competitive advantages (we'll explain this concept more in a bit).

Since the majority of excess return is added in higher-level decisions in the top-down process, it's not vital to pick the "best" stocks in the universe. Rather, you want to pick stocks with a good probability of outperforming their peers. Doing so can enhance returns without jeopardizing good top-down decisions by picking risky, go-big-or-go-home stocks. Being right more often than not should create outperformance relative to the benchmark over time.

A FIVE-STEP PROCESS

Analyzing a stock against its peer group can be summarized as a five-step process:

1. Understand business and earnings drivers
2. Identify strategic attributes
3. Analyze fundamental and stock price performance
4. Identify risks
5. Analyze valuations and consensus expectations

These five steps provide a consistent framework for analyzing firms in their peer groups. While these steps are far from a full stock analysis, they provide the basics necessary to begin making better stock selections.

Step 1: Understand Business and Earnings Drivers

The first step is to understand what the business does, how it generates its earnings, and what drives those earnings. Here are a few tips to help in the process.

Industry overview: Begin any analysis with a basic understanding of the firm's industry, including its drivers and risks. You should be familiar with how current economic trends affect the industry.

- **Company description.** Obtain a business description of the company, including an understanding of the products and services within each business segment. It's always best to go directly to a company's financial statements for this. (Almost every public firm makes its financial statements readily accessible online these days.) Browse the firm's website and financial statements/reports to gain an overview of the company and how it presents itself.
- **Corporate history.** Read the firm's history since its inception and especially over the last several years. An understanding of firm history may reveal its growth strategy or consistency with success and failure. It also will provide clues on what its true core competencies are. Ask questions like: Has it been an industry leader for decades, or is it a relative newcomer? Has it switched strategies or businesses often in the past?
- **Business segments.** Break down company revenues and earnings by business segment and geography to determine how and where it makes its money. Find out what drives results in each business and geographic segment. Begin thinking about how each of these business segments fits into your high-level themes.
- **Recent news/press releases.** Read all recently released news about the stock, including press releases. Do a Google search and see what comes up. Look for any significant announcements regarding company operations. What is the media's opinion of the firm? Is it a bellwether to the industry or a minor player?
- **Markets and customers.** Identify main customers and the markets it operates in. Determine whether the firm has any particularly large single customer or a concentrated customer base.
- **Competition.** Find the main competitors and how market share compares with other industry players. Is the industry highly segmented? Assess the industry's competitive landscape. Keep in mind the biggest competitors can sometimes lurk in

different industries—sometimes even in different sectors! Get a feel for how the firm stacks up—is it an industry leader or a minor player? Does market share matter in that industry?

Step 2: Identify Strategic Attributes

After gaining a firm grasp of company operations, the next step is identifying strategic attributes consistent with higher-level portfolio themes. Also known as competitive or comparative advantages, strategic attributes are unique features allowing firms to outperform their industry or sector. Since industry peers are generally affected by the same high-level drivers, strong strategic attributes are the edge in creating superior performance. Examples of strategic attributes include:

- High relative market share
- Low-cost production
- Superior sales relationships/distribution
- Economic sensitivity
- Vertical integration
- Strong management/business strategy
- Geographic diversity or advantage
- Consolidator
- Strong balance sheet
- Niche market exposure
- Pure play
- Potential takeover target
- Proprietary technologies
- Strong brand name
- First mover advantage

Portfolio drivers help determine which strategic attributes are likely to face head- or tailwinds. After all, not all strategic attributes will benefit a firm in all environments. For example, Managed Health Care companies with high US government exposure benefited from the expansion of Medicare in the early part of the decade, but it could

Strategic Attributes: Making Lemonade

How do strategic attributes help you analyze individual stocks? Consider a simple example: There are five lemonade stands of similar size, product, and quality within a city block. A scorching heat wave envelops the city, sending a rush of customers in search of lemonade. Which stand benefits most from the industry-wide surge in business? This likely depends on each stand's strategic attributes. Maybe one is a cost leader and has cheapest access to homegrown lemons. Maybe one has a geographic advantage and is located next to a basketball court full of thirsty players. Or maybe one has a superior business strategy with a "buy two, get one free" initiative that drives higher sales volume and a bigger customer base. Any of these are core strategic advantages.

have the opposite effect if the government cuts Medicare reimbursements. Thus, it's essential to pick strategic attributes consistent with higher-level portfolio themes.

A strategic attribute is also only effective to the extent management recognizes and takes advantage of it. Execution is key. For example, if a firm's strategic attribute is technological expertise, it should focus its effort on research and development to maintain that edge. If its strategic attribute is low-cost production relative to its peer group, it should capitalize by potentially lowering prices or expanding production (assuming the new production is also low cost) to gain market share.

Identifying strategic attributes may require thorough research of the firm's financial statements, website, news stories, history, and discussions with customers, suppliers, competitors, and management. Don't skimp on this step—be diligent and thorough in finding strategic attributes. It may feel an arduous task at times, but it's also among the most important in security selection.

Step 3: Analyze Fundamental and Stock Price Performance

Once you've gained a thorough understanding of the business, earnings drivers, and strategic attributes, the next step is analyzing firm performance both fundamentally and in the stock market.

Using the latest earnings releases and annual report, analyze company performance in recent quarters. Ask:

- What are recent revenue trends? Earnings? Margins? Which business segments are seeing rising or falling sales?
- Is the firm growing its business organically, because of acquisitions, or for some other reason?
- How sustainable is its strategy?
- Are earnings growing because of strong demand or because of cost cutting?
- Is the firm using tax loopholes and one-time items?
- What is management's strategy to grow the business for the future?
- What is the financial health of the company?
- Not all earnings results are created equal. Understanding what drives results gives clues to what will drive future performance.

Check the company's stock chart for the last few years and try to determine what has driven performance. Explain any big up or down moves and identify any significant news events. If the stock price has trended steadily downward despite consistently beating earnings estimates, there may be a force driving the whole industry downward, like expectations for lower Health Care Supplies prices. Likewise, if the company's stock soared despite reporting tepid earnings growth or prospects, there may be some force driving the industry higher, like takeover speculation. Or stocks can simply move in sympathy with the broader market. Whatever it is, make sure you know.

After reading the earnings calls of a firm and its peers (these are typically posted on the investor relations section of a firm's website every quarter and transcripts can also be found at http://seekingalpha .com/tag/transcripts), you'll begin to notice similar trends and events affecting the industry. Take note of these so you can distinguish between issues that are company-specific or industry wide. For example, regulatory and legislative policies can impact the entire Pharmaceuticals industry, but patent expirations and pipeline development may only affect specific companies.

Step 4: Identify Risks

There are two main types of risks in security analysis: stock-specific risks and systematic risks (also known as non–stock specific risks). Both can be equally important to performance.

Stock-specific risks, as the name suggests, are issues affecting the company in isolation. These are mainly risks affecting a firm's business operations or future operations. Some company-specific risks are discussed in detail in the annual reports, 10-Ks for US firms and the 20-Fs for foreign filers (found at www.sec.gov). But one can't rely solely on firms' self-identifying risk factors. You must see what analysts are saying about them and identify all risks for yourself. Some examples include:

- Important patent expirations or patents being challenged
- Customer concentration
- Product concentration
- Sole suppliers
- Excessive leverage or lack of access to financing
- Obsolete products
- Weak pipeline
- Competitive environment
- Poor operational track record, including ability to integrate acquired companies
- High operating costs versus competitors and historical averages
- Late Securities and Exchange Commission (SEC) filings
- Financial statements that are difficult to understand
- Qualified audit opinions
- Pension or benefit underfunding risk
- Legal issues (e.g., pending litigation)
- Pending corporate actions
- Executive departures
- Stock ownership concentration (insider or institutional) and method of acquisition
- Regional political/governmental risk

Systematic risks include macroeconomic or geopolitical events out of a company's control. While the risks may affect a broad set of firms, they will have varying effects on each. Some examples include:

- Geopolitical and regulatory risks
- Legislation affecting taxes, royalties, or subsidies
- Economic activity
- Interest rates
- Currency
- Capital expenditures
- Industry cost inflation
- Strained supply chain
- Commodity prices

Identifying stock-specific risks helps an investor evaluate the relative risk and reward potential of firms within a peer group. Identifying systematic risks helps you make informed decisions about which sub-industries and countries to overweight or underweight.

If you don't feel strongly about any company in a peer group within a sub-industry you wish to overweight, you could pick the company with the least stock-specific risk. This would help to achieve the goal of picking firms with the greatest probability of outperforming their peer groups but still performing in line with your higher-level themes and drivers.

Step 5: Analyze Valuations and Consensus Expectations

Valuations can be tricky. They are tools used to evaluate market sentiment and expectations for firms. They are not a foolproof way to determine whether a stock is "cheap" or "expensive." Valuations are primarily used to compare firms against their peer group (or peer average) or a company's valuation relative to its own history. As mentioned earlier, stocks move not on the expected, but the unexpected. We aim to try and gauge what the consensus expects for a company's future performance and then assess whether that company will perform below, in line, or above expectations.

Valuations provide little information by themselves in predicting future stock performance. Just because one company's P/E is 20 while another's is 10 doesn't mean you should buy the one at 10 because it's "cheaper." There's likely a reason why one company has a different valuation than another, including such things as strategic attributes, earnings expectations, sentiment, stock-specific risks, and management's reputation. The main usefulness of valuations is explaining why a company's valuation differs from its peers and determining if it's justified.

There are many different valuation metrics investors use in security analysis. Some of the most popular include:

- P/E—price-to-earnings
- P/FE—price-to-forward earnings
- P/B—price-to-book
- P/S—price-to-sales
- P/CF—price-to-cash-flow
- DY—dividend yield
- EV/EBITDA—enterprise value to earnings before interest, taxes, depreciation, and amortization

Once you've compiled the valuations for a peer group, try to estimate why there are relative differences and if they're justified. Is a company's relatively low valuation due to stock-specific risk or low confidence from investors? Is the company's forward P/E relatively high because consensus is wildly optimistic about the stock? A firm's higher valuation may be entirely justified, for example, if it has a growth rate greater than its peers. A lower valuation may be warranted for a company facing a challenging operating environment in which it is losing market share. Seeing valuations in this way will help to differentiate firms and spot potential opportunities or risks.

Valuations should be used in combination with previous analysis of a company's fundamentals, strategic attributes, and risks. For example, Figure 8.1 is a grid showing how an investor could combine an analysis of strategic attributes and valuations to help pick firms.

Figure 8.1   Strategic Attributes and Valuation

Stocks with relatively low valuations but attractive strategic attributes may be underappreciated by the market (as shown in Figure 8.1). Stocks with relatively high valuations but no discernible strategic attributes may be overvalued by the market. Either way, use valuations appropriately and in the context of a larger investment opinion about a stock, not as a panacea for true value.

IMPORTANT QUESTIONS TO ASK

While this chapter's framework can be used to analyze any firm, there are additional factors specific to the Health Care sector that must be considered. The following section provides some of the most important factors and questions to consider when researching firms in the sector. Answers to these questions should help distinguish between firms within a peer group and help identify strategic attributes and stock-specific risks. While there are countless other questions and factors that could and should be asked when researching Health Care firms, these should serve as a good starting point.

Product mix. Well-positioned firms maintain strong market share positions in a variety of products and in growing categories. How diversified is the firm's revenue base? What are the key products and their corresponding growth rates? Is it highly exposed to a single product? How does this compare to competitors? How are its products and services differentiated?

Business strategy. Has the company recently been acquiring or divesting businesses? If so, what are the drivers behind such activity? If the company is a consolidator, does it have a successful track record of creating positive synergies like increased purchasing power, capacity utilization, and distribution network efficiencies? When it comes to acquisitions, you should also investigate risks such as brand dilution and overpaying. You want to know how long it takes for the average deal to be accretive to the bottom line. If a firm is in divestment mode, what were the catalysts, and what is the strategy looking forward? Is it moving into higher growth categories? Is the company a turnaround story? If so, what is the estimated timetable for execution?

Geographic diversity. How wide is the firm's geographic reach? Does the firm have meaningful exposure to high-growth international markets? Is the firm concentrated in a slow-growth, mature market? Geographic diversification can help smooth earnings trends because growth in one market can offset weakness in other markets. If a company is expanding internationally, what do margins look like in those markets? What are the capital expenditure requirements to build manufacturing and distribution abroad? What is the ROI (return on investment), and how long is the estimated payoff? For internationally diversified firms, keep in mind that fluctuations in foreign currency values influence the way sales and earnings are reported in US dollars.

Input costs. What are the firm's primary input costs, how have they been trending, and what impact might they have on the firm's margins? Does the company have pricing power to pass through rising input costs? What's driving margin expansion or contraction? Does it hedge certain costs or risk exposures, such as currency or commodities? If it does hedge, how effective has it been in the past? Oftentimes, monitoring commodity prices requires also monitoring weather patterns, which can have a large impact on supply levels for many commodities.

Competition and barriers to entry. What does the competitive landscape look like? Does the firm operate in a fragmented industry or a concentrated industry? Are there firmly entrenched market share leaders who are insulated from smaller competitors via high barriers to entry? Are there substitutes for the company's products or services? If market share changes rapidly, what prompts those changes historically? Is the industry prone to quick-changing fads or is the landscape slow to change? High barriers to entry typically provide pricing power and reduce competition.

Power of buyers and suppliers. Does the company have large exposure to a particular customer or supplier? Many times, governments and group purchasing organizations are large buyers and account for a significant portion of a company's sales—they have power to influence pricing and costs.

Innovation. New product development is crucial in sustaining healthy, long-term, organic growth. To analyze innovation potential for the future, you should look foremost at the firm's track record. How successful has it been in pioneering new products versus its peers? Is it producing new innovative products, "me too" products, or next-generation products? How much does the firm spend annually on R&D as a percentage of sales? Is this ratio consistent? Declining R&D investment can result in slowing future organic growth as new breakthrough products are more difficult to develop.

Sales growth. Net sales growth is a positive sign for a business, but as a stock analyst, you must determine how top-line sales growth is derived if you are to determine the quality of the sales growth. Was the top line influenced primarily by acquisitions or divestitures, or was it organic growth from ongoing operations? Is the market in which it operates increasing or shrinking? You can extrapolate organic growth into the future with more confidence than you can with acquisition-based growth, so it is generally considered a more relevant analytic.

After you've broken out organic growth, the next question becomes how was that growth achieved? Was it driven through pricing? Increasing unit volume? Analyze whether the firm is growing primarily through one or the other. While price increases are generally a positive, they can be destructive if they lead to volume deterioration, resulting in market share loss. Ideally, a firm will demonstrate strong volume growth along with pricing power, particularly during periods when input costs are accelerating.

Management. What is management's reputation? Is a seasoned team in place with a strong track record of building the business and adding shareholder value? Have they executed on stated goals and met their guidance to Wall Street? Has there been management turnover? Does the firm promote from within or look outside the company for its senior leadership? What is management's policy relative to free cash flow management—are they buying back shares, increasing dividends, or reinvesting in the business? Does management clearly articulate its business strategy and directly answer questions? Some executive teams are particularly adept at containing costs, while others are known experts at facilitating new product development and managing expansion. Is the board of directors largely independent or is there cronyism? Investigate what management's perceived strengths and weaknesses are, and evaluate whether the right people are at the helm to lead the company in a positive direction.

Brand equity. Is the product highly recognizable and respected? What are the firm's strategies in promoting the brand? A well-respected brand gives a firm the ability to price its product above the competition, deflect substitution effects, and deliver superior profits to investors.

Sales relationships and distribution. How does the firm's distribution platform compare to the rest of the industry? Is the sales staff growing or shrinking? Is the target market becoming wider or smaller? Is the sales force targeting doctors or payers (e.g., government and insurance)? Does the firm have an internal sales force or rely on a third party? Are there any cost advantages or disadvantages to these approaches?

Regulation. How are the firm's operations affected by regulation? Does the firm currently operate in a favorable regulatory environment? How might that change? With ever-present concerns surrounding health care safety, the regulatory environment is particularly important to bio-pharmaceutical and equipment companies. Monitor whether the firm has incurred recalls or warnings (e.g., black box warnings) of any sort as a result of government or safety group investigations.

Geopolitical/legislation risks. Health care and politics are closely tied together, and legislative changes can happen on a relatively frequent basis. Questions to consider are how does new legislation impact reimbursements, pricing, patents, taxes, litigation, competition, labor, subsidies, and tariffs? Some countries have been known to de-recognize patents and nationalize assets, so it's important to know the company's global exposure and growth plans.

Margins. Are margins growing or shrinking, and what is driving this movement? Has the company historically offset higher costs with higher prices? How do its margins compare to those of peers?

Be mindful company management can manipulate the income statement to make margins appear more favorable. Manipulation can take many forms, but a few include reducing sales reserves/return estimates to boost net sales, booking revenues early to increase sales, excessively increasing production to expand gross margins, and temporarily cutting R&D and SG&A spending to boost operating margins.

Expense items should be studied individually and carefully via the income statement. Line items such as SG&A and R&D costs should be analyzed in relation to industry norms.

Specific to Managed Care, it is important to understand the level, trend, and comparison of its medical loss ratio (MLR). Refer to Chapter 5 for an in-depth discussion of the MLR.

Margins are particularly important in an environment with rising raw material prices. The more commoditized the firm's end market, the less pricing power it typically controls, which can lead to negative earnings during periods of sharply rising input costs. Conversely, strong brand equity and uniquely differentiated products facilitate pricing power, which can stabilize margins during periods of inflation.

Financial strength. Does the company have enough cash and cash flows to operate well into the future? Compare the firm's interest costs with the amount of operating income the business generates (interest coverage ratio). Will the firm require additional funds in the future to expand its operation? If so, is there capacity to take on more debt, or would the firm have to engage in an equity offering that might dilute existing shareholders? You can investigate financial health by comparing balance sheet financial ratios to a firm's peers. Ratios such as long-term debt-to-capital and the current ratio can be used to assess a firm's capitalization structure and level of liquidity. Comparing credit ratings to peers is another tool at your disposal. The primary credit agencies include Standard & Poor's, Moody's, and Fitch.

Recall debt isn't necessarily a bad thing when defining financial strength—many firms generate an excellent return on borrowed funds. Understanding the capital structure of a firm and its history of generating returns on capital will help you appraise the optimal level of debt.

Outlook. After answering the questions above and combining them with your knowledge of the industry, you should be prepared to determine a firm's future prospects. Not only is it important to determine if prospects are favorable or not, but consider if your assessment is already reflected in valuations and share price performance. What are analysts and media saying about the stock? Are valuations above or below those of peers and its own historical averages? If you think a firm's prospects aren't appealing but shares are trading at a substantial discount to peers and itself, poor sentiment is most likely already reflected in the share price, and it could be an opportune time to invest in the stock.

Chapter Recap

Security analysis is not nearly as complicated as it seems. In the top-down investment process, stocks are essentially tools we use to take advantage of opportunities we identify in higher-level themes. Once an attractive segment of the market is identified, we attempt to determine the firms most likely to outperform their peers by finding firms with strategic attributes. While the five-step security selection process is just one of many ways to research firms, it is an effective framework for selecting securities within the top-down process.

- Do not limit yourself to the questions provided in this chapter when researching Health Care firms—they are just some tools to help you distinguish between firms. The more questions you ask, the better your analysis will be.
- Stock selection, the third and final step in the top-down investment process, attempts to identify securities that will benefit from our high-level portfolio themes.
- Ultimately, stock selection attempts to spot opportunities not currently discounted into prices.
- To identify firms most likely to outperform their peer group, we must find firms that possess competitive advantages (aka, strategic attributes).
- A five-step security selection process can be used as a framework to research firms.
- Firms within each industry have specific characteristics and strategies separating potential winners from losers. Asking the right questions can help identify those features.

MAKE YOUR PORTFOLIO "HEALTHY"

Now it's time to transfer our Health Care sector knowledge and analysis into strategy. In this chapter, we discuss various Health Care investment strategies, including examples of when to overweight and underweight industries and sub-industries throughout a market cycle. The strategies include:

- Adding value at the industry and sub-industry level
- Adding value at the security level
- Adding value in a Health Care sector downturn

As covered so far, fundamentals can differ widely by sub-industry, so overweight and underweight decisions in each area are vital for success. Remember, we're investing within the context of a top-down model (if you need a refresher, revisit Chapter 7). So we'll be talking less about specific stocks and more about overweighting industries and sub-industries that should benefit if higher-level themes play out as expected.

While the strategies presented here are by no means comprehensive, they provide a good starting point for constructing a portfolio that can increase your likelihood of outperforming a Health Care benchmark. They should also help spur some investment strategy ideas of your own. After all, using this framework to discover information few others have yet to discover is what investing is all about.

STRATEGY 1: ADDING VALUE AT THE INDUSTRY AND SUB-INDUSTRY LEVEL

The first strategy is overweighting and underweighting Health Care industries or sub-industries based on your market outlook and analysis (e.g., the top-down method). Within the Health Care sector, each industry and sub-industry can fall in and out of favor frequently—no one area outperforms consistently over the long term. Each will lead or lag depending on drivers like regulation, pipeline development, patent expirations, government spending, production costs, and global or regional growth in end markets.

A look at the performance of the S&P 500 Health Care industries from 1995 to 2009 (Table 9.1) illustrates the variability of returns. Calendar year industry total returns are compared to the Health Care sector total returns. Shaded regions highlight industry outperformance.

The fundamentals, themes, and drivers covered in this book can be seen throughout the time period. Notably:

1. Pharmaceuticals outperformed from 1995 to 1998 as companies launched a multitude of blockbuster drugs like cholesterol treatment Lipitor.
2. Biotechnology performed relatively well from 1995 to 2005 as the industry launched innovative drugs to treat complex diseases like cancer and HIV/AIDS.
3. Equipment & Supplies performed relatively well from 1999 to 2004 with rapid uptake of orthopedic implants and the launch of key products like cardiac rhythm management devices and drug-eluting stents.

Table 9.1   S&P 500 Health Care Industry Total Returns

Date	Health Care Sector	Pharma	Biotech	Equipment & Supplies	Providers & Services	Life Sciences	Health Care Tech
1995	58.0%	60.1%	101.3%	63.0%	33.1%	NA	NA
1996	21.0%	25.5%	−8.4%	15.1%	7.3%	NA	NA
1997	43.7%	53.6%	−0.5%	21.8%	7.8%	NA	NA
1998	43.9%	49.0%	93.2%	43.5%	−8.6%	NA	NA
1999	−10.7%	−12.0%	129.8%	−4.9%	−37.2%	NA	NA
2000	37.1%	36.3%	−4.8%	44.1%	76.0%	NA	NA
2001	−11.9%	−14.5%	−3.7%	−5.1%	−3.0%	NA	NA
2002	−18.8%	−20.0%	−20.4%	−12.5%	−13.5%	NA	NA
2003	15.1%	8.8%	28.9%	32.2%	23.8%	NA	NA
2004	1.7%	−7.4%	7.6%	12.9%	23.0%	NA	NA
2005	6.5%	−3.4%	18.3%	0.5%	34.5%	NA	NA
2006	7.5%	15.9%	−2.7%	3.9%	−2.1%	NA	NA
2007	7.2%	4.7%	−3.4%	5.4%	20.0%	23.3%	−15.8%
2008	−22.8%	−18.2%	10.3%	−27.5%	−44.1%	−39.0%	−33.8%
2009	19.7%	18.6%	−7.3%	28.7%	36.3%	57.4%	40.2%
Average Annual Return	**13.1%**	**13.1%**	**22.5%**	**14.7%**	**10.2%**	**13.9%**	**23.1%**
Cumulative Return	**358.8%**	**331.8%**	**836.3%**	**471.6%**	**139.5%**	**18.4%**	**221.9%**
Standard Deviation	**24.4%**	**26.9%**	**46.4%**	**24.3%**	**30.5%**	**48.9%**	**38.6%**

Note: 2007 was the first full year the Life Sciences and Health Care Tech industries were separately classified.
Source: Thomson Reuters; MSCI, Inc.[1] 12/31/1994–12/31/2009.

4. Providers & Services produced strong returns from 2001 to 2006 as the expansion of Medicare and declining unemployment levels drove membership and profit growth.

Ultimately, your decision to overweight or underweight a subindustry relative to the benchmark should be consistent with your high-level portfolio drivers. Based on the themes and drivers covered throughout this book, you should now have an understanding of the fundamentals driving stock market returns and the tools to track them moving forward. Note: *Always remember past performance is no guarantee of future performance.* No set of rules works for all time, and you should always analyze the entire situation before investing—starting with expectations of how supply and demand may shift. The past is about understanding context and precedent for investing—it's not a road map for the future.

How to Implement Sub-Asset Allocation Over- and Underweights

Once you've evaluated a sector's fundamentals and formed opinions about expected returns, follow these two steps to implement industry or sub-industry allocation over- and underweights:

1. Determine the weight relative to your benchmark's weight in that category. The size of your relative bet should be proportional to your conviction. When you have only mild conviction, make a modest bet against the benchmark. When you believe you have significant information others don't have or interpret the same information everyone else has differently, make a bigger bet. But never make a bet so large that, if you're wrong, will inflict irreparable damage on your portfolio's return versus the benchmark.

2. Determine how you plan to fill out the allocation. You have several alternatives: If you don't feel you have any useful security-specific insights, you might simply buy all the stocks in that category. Or you might buy some representative stocks, perhaps either the biggest or those with the highest correlation to the category. Or you might buy an exchange-traded fund (ETF) or mutual fund that encompasses the category. (For more information on available ETFs, visit www.ishares.com, www.sectorspdr.com, or www.masterdata.com.) Or you might try to add additional value with security selection strategies.

Industry and Sub-Industry Cheat Sheet

Sectors and their components are dynamic, and fundamentals change over time. For reference, however, here's a quick cheat sheet with pointers on each industry and sub-industry.

Pharmaceuticals

- Pharmaceuticals makes up a significant portion of most major Health Care indexes, so it's a good idea to hold at least a small allocation of it in any Health Care portfolio to reduce benchmark risk.
- Drivers include R&D pipeline progression, demographics, legislation and regulation, pricing, product performance, drug safety profile, and patent exclusivity.
- The industry is operationally a high-risk/high-reward business because drug development is extremely expensive and most drug developments fail. However, the few commercially successful drugs are very profitable and more than offset the failed ones.
- Large pharmaceutical companies are generally characterized as highly profitable with low financial leverage, and their stocks' performance is typically less volatile than the broader market because their diversified product portfolios and stable demand generally make for stable operations.
- Small firms are generally characterized as higher beta/higher risk because they often have little or no product sales, are not profitable, and future prospects rely on pipeline development of one or a few products.
- Pharmaceutical companies are located around the world.

Biotechnology

- The Biotechnology industry is similar to the Pharmaceuticals industry in terms of characteristics, drivers, and risk profiles of large and small firms.
- Drivers include R&D pipeline progression, demographics, legislation and regulation, pricing, product performance, drug safety profile, and patent exclusivity.
- Biotech is dominated by a few companies, and its index weight is generally much smaller than the Pharmaceuticals industry.
- Small firms are generally characterized as higher beta/higher risk because they often have little or no product sales, are not profitable, and future prospects rely on pipeline development of one or a few products.
- Most of the larger publicly traded Biotech companies are located in the US.

(Continued)

Equipment & Supplies

Equipment

- This fragmented sub-industry primarily focuses on high-tech products serving specific end markets like cardiovascular, orthopedics, or neuromodulation.
- Several of the largest Equipment companies are divisions of larger conglomerates outside the Health Care sector.
- Growth is driven by a successful R&D pipeline, demographics, legislation and regulation, increased hospital reimbursements, product performance, safety profile, pricing, patent expirations, and general economic trends.
- Relative to the bio-pharmaceuticals industry, this sub-industry has weaker patent protection, and the intense nature of product development can quickly render existing products obsolete.
- Equipment tends to be more economically sensitive because recessions can either cause hospitals to reduce equipment spending or pressure pricing. A weak economy can also delay elective procedures like knee replacements or plastic surgery.
- Most of the larger publicly traded Equipment firms are based in the US.

Supplies

- The Supplies sub-industry is dominated by low-tech equipment and supply providers of products like rubber gloves, tables, and stethoscopes.
- There are many small players located throughout the world.
- Unless you have great conviction in your beliefs, it is unlikely you'll want to hold a significant weight due to benchmark risk.

Providers & Services

Managed Health Care

- The sub-industry is dominated by a few companies.
- Growth is driven by increased membership, stable or declining health care costs, investment portfolio performance, and government reimbursement levels.
- Managed Care stocks are primarily US-based companies.
- Unless you have great conviction in your beliefs, it is unlikely you'll want to hold a significant weight due to benchmark risk.

Services

- The sub-industry is dominated by a few pharmacy benefit managers and laboratory testing companies.
- Pharmacy benefit manager growth is driven by increased prescription use, and generic drugs carry higher margins for the benefit managers.
- Unless you have great conviction in your beliefs, it is unlikely you'll want to hold a significant weight due to benchmark risk.

Facilities

- The sub-industry is characterized by many small regional facilities like hospitals and rehabilitation centers.
- Growth is driven by government reimbursements, regional population growth, economic trends, and patient enrollments.
- Unless you have great conviction in your beliefs, it is unlikely you'll want to hold a significant weight due to benchmark risk.

Distributors

- The sub-industry is dominated by a few large US firms, with many smaller distributors located around the world.
- Demand is driven by hospital expansion and ability to secure or renew distribution contracts. Pharmaceuticals consolidation could pressure pricing power and reduce distributor profits.
- Unless you have great conviction in your beliefs, it is unlikely you'll want to hold a significant weight due to benchmark risk.

Life Sciences Tools & Services

- The sub-industry is dominated by small companies.
- Growth is driven by bio-pharmaceutical R&D spending, academic research, government funding, and industrial usage (e.g., food, water, and air testing).
- Life Sciences can be more economically sensitive—a slowing economy can drive hospitals, companies, schools, and governments to reduce equipment spending.
- Most of the larger Life Sciences firms are based in the US.

(Continued)

- Unless you have great conviction in your beliefs, it's unlikely you'll want to hold a significant weight due to benchmark risk.

Health Care Technology

- The small size of this sub-industry renders its benchmark importance relatively meaningless.
- Growth is driven by industry need to upgrade technology and push toward electronic health records and commerce.
- Unless you have great conviction in your beliefs, it's unlikely you'll want to hold a significant weight due to benchmark risk.

STRATEGY 2: ADDING VALUE AT THE SECURITY LEVEL

A more advanced strategy entails investing in firms within a sub-industry based on a specific business mix. This strategy could be based on different opinions about specific end markets, regions, government exposure, growth prospects, patent expirations, or some combination of all the above. For example, if you think generic drug demand will outperform branded pharmaceutical demand in the near future, you could:

- Buy generic manufacturers and sell short Pharmaceuticals.
- Overweight PBMs and underweight Pharmaceuticals.

These are just a couple of examples. Countless other tactics could be employed within sub-industries. As you become more familiar with specific Health Care firms and their industries, you can eventually develop your own strategies. Always be vigilant for company-specific issues that could cause a stock to act differently than you would expect in the context of your broader strategy. (And be sure to revisit Chapter 8 for tips on how to select individual stocks.)

STRATEGY 3: ADDING VALUE IN A HEALTH CARE SECTOR DOWNTURN

Most of this book focused on what drives the Health Care sector and its industries forward. But what could cause a Health Care boom to bust?

No one sector or industry can outperform forever. The stock market eventually sniffs out all opportunities for excess returns, and sector leadership changes. So it's important to continually review all the drivers and question your high-level portfolio themes regularly.

A downturn in the Health Care sector could be triggered by a decline in global GDP, falling corporate profits, and reduced government or insurance reimbursements. While there are countless reasons why this could happen, here are a few possible examples that could negatively impact the sector:

- Recession—regional or global; perceived or real
- Negative demographic changes
- Lower capital expenditures
- Weak pipeline
- Increased competition/substitution
- Restrictive legislative or regulatory environment
- Patent expirations
- Increased product or industry risk profile
- Obsolete products
- Weakening corporate profitability
- Higher costs of capital
- Overly bullish sentiment causing a speculative bubble

Should your analysis lead you to believe the next 12 months will be a bad time for Health Care stocks—because of the reasons above or something else—then it may be appropriate to either reduce or eliminate your weight in Health Care firms or adopt a defensive position in the portfolio.

HOW TO IMPLEMENT YOUR STRATEGY

Let's briefly look at a few examples of how to implement these strategies in a portfolio. If you expect an industry to outperform relative to the benchmark and want to overweight it, you can use what you learned in Chapter 8 to pick stocks likely to outperform their peers.

But if you don't want to do that heavy of an analysis on individual stocks, you could purchase the largest stocks in the industry in an attempt to mimic it. You can often create a good proxy that acts very similarly to the industry's performance as a whole just by owning the largest stocks. For example, Pfizer, one of the largest companies in the S&P 500 Pharmaceuticals Index as of December 31, 2009, had a monthly correlation of 0.81 to the S&P 500 Pharmaceuticals Index from 2005 through 2009.[2]

You can also use ETFs to gain broad exposure to an industry or the entire sector. For example, the iShares Dow Jones US Health Care Sector Fund (ticker: IYH) and iShares S&P Global Health Care Sector Fund (ticker: IXJ) are designed to track sector-level performance. The iShares Dow Jones US Medical Devices Index Fund (ticker: IHI) is designed to track medical equipment companies on an industry level, while the NASDAQ Biotechnology Index Fund (ticker: IBB) is meant to track Biotechnology and Life Sciences companies. (Note: These are just a few examples of securities designed to track industries. Further research should be done for more investment options. More information can be found at www.masterdata.com, which provides a list of ETFs.)

The smaller the industry or sub-industry, however, the less likely it is that an ETF exists to track the exposure you desire. If using ETFs, always be sure to investigate underlying holdings to ensure they track the actual region, index, or sub-industry you want. If you are using a global index as your benchmark, a US-only Health Care ETF is unlikely to closely track the returns of the Health Care sector in your benchmark.

If you have lower expectations for the sector, you can simply underweight by selling stock or reducing your ETF weight. You can even short individual securities or ETFs in an attempt to capitalize on a sector you suspect will underperform. But shorting is a more sophisticated strategy, as is using margin or options (which can be used either to augment an over- or underweight). Because of the potential leverage involved, such strategies should only be used by sophisticated investors.

If you're outright bearish on the entire industry or stocks in general, a simple strategy is to hold cash/bonds. Keep in mind—such a strategy is far riskier than it sounds. This is seriously deviating from your benchmark, and you run the risk of being wrong and missing equity-like upside. But should you be confident in your bearish forecast, you can again short stocks or ETFs, buy reverse ETFs, and use options in an attempt to get better than cash- or bond-like returns.

Because of the potential leverage involved, strategies involving options (which can be used either to augment an over- or underweight), futures, and margin should *only* be used by sophisticated investors. Shorting is also a more sophisticated strategy. Significant deviations from your benchmark should only take place when you have a strong conviction that you know something others do not.

If you're willing and able to increase your risk exposure, another strategy involves the use of private equity and venture capital funds that specialize in the Health Care industry. These strategies can materially increase your return potential, but they also have the potential to cause severe losses because often they invest in start-up companies and can use heavy amounts of financial leverage. If you consider this option, it is important to fully understand the firm you are hiring, including the manager's strategy, track record, fee schedule, use of leverage, lock-up period, and fund minimums.

For most investors, it's usually best to stick to a straightforward strategy of using ETFs and single stocks to over- and underweight industries and sub-industries based on your forecast.

Chapter Recap

We couldn't possibly list every investment strategy out there for this dynamic sector. Different strategies will work best at different times. Some will become obsolete. New ones will be discovered. Whatever strategies you choose, *always know you could be wrong!* Decisions to significantly overweight or underweight a sub-industry relative to the benchmark, using shorting or options strategies, or general speculation should be

(Continued)

based on a multitude of factors, including an assessment of risk. The point of bench-marking is to properly diversify, so make sure you always have counterstrategies built into your portfolio.

- There are numerous ways to invest in the Health Care sector. These include invest-ing directly in stocks or indirectly through mutual funds, ETFs, or derivatives.
- Investors can enhance returns by overweighting and underweighting Health Care sub-industries based on a variety of high-level drivers.
- An advanced strategy involves making bets on firms with different business lines within sub-industries, like buying a Health Care Equipment company that focuses on orthopedics and shorting another that focuses on cardiovascular treatment.
- There are countless reasons Health Care could underperform, including negative leg-islative and regulatory changes, demographic changes, and economic developments.

Appendix
Reference Material

GOVERNMENT

United States

Department of Health and Human Services (www.hhs.gov/)

> The HHS is the health care regulatory body of the United States. The website provides useful health care information.

Food and Drug Administration (www.fda.gov/)

> The FDA is an agency of the Department of Health and Human Services. It's responsible for regulating and supervising food, prescription, and over-the-counter pharmaceutical medicine, medical devices, tobacco, and other health-related products and services.

National Institutes of Health (www.nih.gov/)

> The NIH is a department of HHS that is responsible for health-related research and funding.

Centers for Medicare and Medicaid Services (www.cms.gov/)

> The Centers for Medicare and Medicaid Services is an HHS agency that administers Medicare, Medicaid, and State Children's Health Insurance Programs.

National Center for Health Statistics (www.cdc.gov/nchs/)

> The NCHS is the nation's principal health statistics agency.

HealthCare.Gov (www.healthcare.gov/)

> HealthCare.Gov is a federal government website managed by HHS. The website provides information regarding the 2010 health care legislation and helps consumers find insurance coverage.

Japan

Ministry of Health, Labor, and Welfare (www.mhlw.go.jp/english/index.html)

> The Ministry of Health, Labor, and Welfare is the health care regulatory body of Japan.

Germany

Federal Ministry of Health (www.bmg.bund.de/)

> The Federal Ministry of Health is the health care regulatory body of Germany.

France

Ministry of Health and Solidarity (www.sante-sports.gouv.fr/)

> The Ministry of Health and Solidarity is the health care regulatory body of France.

United Kingdom

National Health Service (www.nhs.uk/)

> The NHS is the health care regulatory body of the UK.

National Institute for Health and Clinical Excellence (www.nice.org.uk/)

> NICE provides guidance, sets quality standards, and manages a national database to improve people's health and prevent and treat ill health in the UK.

China

Ministry of Health (www.moh.gov.cn/)

> The Ministry of Health is the health care regulatory body of China.

European Union

European Medicines Agency (www.ema.europa.eu/)

> The EMEA evaluates medicine developed by pharmaceutical companies in the EU.

GLOBAL ORGANIZATIONS

World Health Organization (www.who.int/en/)

> The WHO is the health care authority within the United Nations system. It is responsible for providing leadership on global health matters, shaping the health research agenda, setting norms and standards, articulating evidence-based policy options, providing technical support to countries, and monitoring and assessing health trends.

Organisation for Economic Co-Operation and Development (www.oecd.org)

> The OECD is one of the world's largest publishers in the fields of economics and public policy, including health care. The OECD is one of the world's sources of comparable statistics and economic and social data.

INDUSTRY ORGANIZATIONS

Pharmaceutical Research and Manufacturers of America (www.phrma.org/)

> PhRMA is a leading advocacy group of bio-pharmaceutical companies. It provides helpful industry education and information.

America's Health Insurance Plans (www.ahip.org/)

> AHIP is a national association of insurance companies with the purpose of representing the group's interests on legislative and regulatory matters.

Biotechnology Industry Organization (www.bio.org/)

> BIO is the world's largest biotechnology organization, providing advocacy, business development, and communications services for members worldwide.

Generic Pharmaceutical Association (www.gphaonline.org/)

> The GPhA represents the manufacturers of generic pharmaceutical products.

American Medical Association (www.ama-assn.org/)

> The AMA is a physician organization representing its members on legislative and regulatory matters.

Medical Device Manufacturers Association (www.medicaldevices .org/)

> The MDMA is a national trade association providing educational and advocacy assistance to medical technology companies.

Advanced Medical Technology Association (www.advamed.org/)

> Advamed represents medical device manufacturers on legislative and regulatory issues.

NEWS AND INFORMATIONAL SOURCES

Kaiser Family Foundation (www.kff.org/)

> Kaiser Family Foundation is a nonprofit, private operating foundation focusing on the major health care issues facing the US, as well as the US role in global health policy.

National Institute for Health Care Management (www.nihcm.org/)

> The National Institute for Health Care Management is a foundation that conducts research, policy analysis, and educational activities on a range of health care issues.

Health Affairs (www.healthaffairs.org/)

> *Health Affairs* is the leading journal of health policy thought and research.

Kaiser Health News (www.kaiserhealthnews.org/)

> Kaiser Health News is a nonprofit news organization providing coverage of health care policy and politics.

Medpedia (www.medpedia.com/)

> Medpedia is a relatively new wiki site dedicated to providing broad-based medical information and related news.

IMS Health (www.imshealth.com/)

> IMS Health is the world's leading provider of market intelligence to the Pharmaceutical and Health Care industries. It provides information on prescription trends and generates industry reports and forecasts.

Food and Drug Law Institute (www.fdli.org/)

> The FDLI provides education in the practice of food and drug law and regulation. FDLI's mission relates to the regulatory programs of the Food and Drug Administration as well as the US Department of Agriculture (especially the Food Safety and Inspection Service), Federal Trade Commission, Department of Justice, Environmental Protection Agency, and other federal and state government agencies as they pertain to human and veterinary drugs, biologics and biotechnology products, medical devices, food, and cosmetics.

Notes

Chapter 1: Health Care Basics

1. MSCI. The MSCI information may only be used for your internal use, may not be reproduced or disseminated in any form and may not be used to create any financial instruments or products or any indices. The MSCI information is provided on an "as is" basis and the user of this information assumes the entire risk of any use made of this information. MSCI, each of its affiliates and each other person involved in or related to compiling, computing, or creating any MSCI information (collectively, the "MSCI Parties") expressly disclaims all warranties (including, without limitation, any warranties of originality, accuracy, completeness, timeliness, noninfringement, merchantability, and fitness for a particular purpose) with respect to this information. Without limiting any of the foregoing, in no event shall any MSCI Party have any liability for any direct, indirect, special, incidental, punitive, consequential (including, without limitation, lost profits) or any other damages.
2. Bloomberg Finance L.P., as of 12/31/2009.
3. Ibid.
4. See note 1.
5. Ibid.
6. Ibid.
7. Fisher Investments Research; "OECD Health Data 2010—Frequently Requested Data," Organisation for Economic Co-Operation and Development, www.oecd.org/document/16/0,3343,en_2649_34631_2085200_1_1_1_1,00.html (accessed June 29, 2010).
8. World Bank, "Gross Domestic Product 2008," http://siteresources.worldbank.org/DATASTATISTICS/Resources/GDP.pdf (accessed May 6, /2010).
9. "National Health Expenditure Projections 2009–2019," www.cms.gov/NationalHealthExpendData/downloads/proj2009.pdf (accessed June 29, 2010); "NHE Face Sheet," Centers for Medicare & Medicaid Services, www.cms.gov/NationalHealthExpendData/25_NHE_Fact_Sheet.asp#TopOfPage (accessed June 29, 2010).
10. See note 1.
11. Ibid.

Chapter 2: The US Health Care System

1. PriceWaterhouseCoopers Health Research Institute, "The Price of Excess: Identifying Waste in Healthcare Spending," www.pwc.com/en_CZ/cz/verejna-sprava-zdravotnictvi/prices-of-excess-healthcare-spending.pdf (6, Exhibit 3) (accessed May 6, 2010).
2. Ibid.

3. Centers for Disease Control and Prevention, "FastStats: Health Insurance Coverage," www.cdc.gov/nchs/fastats/hinsure.htm (accessed August 27, 2010).

4. US Census Bureau, "Household Income Rises, Poverty Rate Unchanged, Number of Uninsured Down," www.census.gov/Press-Release/www/releases/archives/income_wealth/012528.html (accessed May 6, 2010).

5. Centers for Medicare and Medicaid Services, "National Health Expenditure Data: NHE Fact Sheet," www.cms.gov/NationalHealthExpendData/25_NHE_Fact_Sheet.asp (accessed May 6, 2010).

6. Ibid.

7. Ibid.

8. Department of Veteran Affairs, "2009 VHA Facility Quality and Safety Report," 7, http://www1.va.gov/health/docs/HospitalReportCard2009.pdf?bcsi_scan_408DE456E3075246=0&bcsi_scan_filename=HospitalReportCard2009.pdf (accessed May 6, 2010).

9. Military Health System, "TRICARE Facts and Figures," www.tricare.mil/pressroom/press_facts.aspx (accessed July 15, 2010).

10. Centers for Medicare and Medicaid Services, "Low Cost Health Insurance for Families & Children," www.cms.gov/LowCostHealthInsFamChild/ (accessed August 27, 2010).

11. WSJ.com, "What's in the Bill," http://online.wsj.com/article/NA_WSJ_PUB:SB10001424052748704117304575137370275522704.html; http://www.kff.org/healthreform/8060.cfm.

Chapter 3: Brief Overview of Health Care Systems by Major Countries

1. World Health Organization, "Health System: China," www.wpro.who.int/countries/2009/chn/national_health_priorities.htm (accessed July 15, 2010).

2. International Monetary Fund, "World Economic Outlook Database, April 2010: Report for Selected Countries and Subjects," www.imf.org/external/pubs/ft/weo/2010/01/weodata/index.aspx (accessed May 17, 2010).

3. Organisation for Economic Co-operation and Development, "OECD Health at a Glance 2009: Key Findings for Japan," www.oecd.org/document/33/0,3343,en_2649_33929_44219681_1_1_1_1,00.html (accessed May 11, 2010).

4. Ibid.

5. "Health Care Around the World: Japan," *Healthcare Economist* (April 17, 2008), http://healthcare-economist.com/2008/04/17/health-care-around-the-world-japan/ (accessed May 11, 2010).

6. Ibid.

7. Organisation for Economic Co-operation and Development, "Health-Care Reform in Japan: Controlling Costs, Improving Quality and Ensuring Equity" (December 4, 2009) 12, www.oecd.org/officialdocuments/displaydocumentpdf/?cote=ECO/WKP(2009)80&doclanguage=en&bcsi_scan_34E336E4D93AA9DD=F/kIR4x1Vi0jKhXQ/FC51CgAAAAKPYwD (accessed August 27, 2010).

8. Organisation for Economic Co-operation and Development, "Health-Care Reform in Japan: Controlling Costs, Improving Quality and Ensuring Equity" (December 4, 2009) 30, www.olis.oecd.org/olis/2009doc.nsf/LinkTo/NT000088AE/$FILE/JT03275812

.PDF?bcsi_scan_23323C003422378C=rw5lrSvNUt0ziCT9OPxYOBAAAADkaHMK &bcsi_scan_filename=JT03275812.PDF (accessed May 11, 2010).

9. See note 2.

10. World Health Organization, "Core Health Indicators," http://apps.who.int/whosis/ database/core/core_select.cfm (accessed May 17, 2010).

11. "The Grass Is Not Always Greener: A Look at National Health Care Systems Around the World," *Policy Analysis,* Cato Institute, 9, www.cato.org/pubs/pas/pa-613.pdf (accessed May 17, 2010).

12. The Federal Association of the AOK, "The AOK in the German Health Care System," 16, www.aok-bv.de/imperia/md/aokbv/aok/aok_flyer_englisch_jan2010_web.pdf (accessed May 17, 2010).

13. Organisation for Economic Co-operation and Development, "OECD Health Data 2009 — Selected Data," http://stats.oecd.org/Index.aspx?DatasetCode=HEALTH (accessed May 17, 2010).

14. See note 2.

15. Ibid.

16. See note 10.

17. "The Grass Is Not Always Greener: A Look at National Health Care Systems Around the World," *Policy Analysis,* Cato Institute, 8, www.cato.org/pubs/pas/pa-613.pdf (accessed May 17, 2010).

18. Ibid.

19. The Henry J. Kaiser Family Foundation, "International Health Systems: Background Brief," www.kaiseredu.org/topics_im_ihs.asp?imID=4&parentID=61 (accessed May 17, 2010).

20. "Salary Snapshot for Family Physician/Doctor Jobs," PayScale, www.payscale.com/ research/US/Job=Family_Physician_%2f_Doctor/Salary (accessed May 17, 2010).

21. See note 11.

22. See note 2.

23. Organisation for Economic Co-operation and Development, "OECD Health at a Glance 2009: Key Findings for the United Kingdom," www.oecd.org/LongAbstract/0,3425, en_ 2649_33929_44220582_70432_119663_1_37407,00.html (accessed May 17, 2010).

24. See note 10.

25. National Health Service, "NHS Jobs," www.jobs.nhs.uk/about_nhs.html (accessed May 17, 2010).

26. Organisation for Economic Co-operation and Development, "OECD Health Data 2010: How Does the United Kingdom Compare," www.oecd.org/dataoecd/46/4/ 38980557.pdf (accessed August 27, 2010).

27. See note 2.

28. World Health Organization, "Measuring Overall Health System Performance for 191 Countries," 20, www.who.int/healthinfo/paper30.pdf

29. See note 2.

30. See note 10.

31. World Health Organization, "Health System," www.wpro.who.int/countries/2009/chn/ national_health_priorities.htm (accessed May 17, 2010).

32. "ISPOR Global Health Care Systems Road Map: Mainland China—Reimbursement Process," International Society for Pharmacoeconomics and Outcomes Research, www .ispor.org/HTARoadMaps/China.asp (accessed June 29, 2010).

33. See note 1.
34. See note 32.

Chapter 4: Health Care Sector Drivers

1. MSCI. The MSCI information may only be used for your internal use, may not be reproduced or disseminated in any form, and may not be used to create any financial instruments or products or any indices. The MSCI information is provided on an "as is" basis, and the user of this information assumes the entire risk of any use made of this information. MSCI, each of its affiliates and each other person involved in or related to compiling, computing or creating any MSCI information (collectively, the "MSCI Parties") expressly disclaims all warranties (including, without limitation, any warranties of originality, accuracy, completeness, timeliness, noninfringement, merchantability, and fitness for a particular purpose) with respect to this information. Without limiting any of the foregoing, in no event shall any MSCI Party have any liability for any direct, indirect, special, incidental, punitive, consequential (including, without limitation, lost profits) or any other damages.

Chapter 5: Health Care Sector Breakdown

1. MSCI. The MSCI information may only be used for your internal use, may not be reproduced or disseminated in any form, and may not be used to create any financial instruments or products or any indices. The MSCI information is provided on an "as is" basis and the user of this information assumes the entire risk of any use made of this information. MSCI, each of its affiliates and each other person involved in or related to compiling, computing or creating any MSCI information (collectively, the "MSCI Parties") expressly disclaims all warranties (including, without limitation, any warranties of originality, accuracy, completeness, timeliness, noninfringement, merchantability and fitness for a particular purpose) with respect to this information. Without limiting any of the foregoing, in no event shall any MSCI Party have any liability for any direct, indirect, special, incidental, punitive, consequential (including, without limitation, lost profits) or any other damages.
2. Ibid.
3. Ibid.
4. Ibid.
5. Ibid.
6. "Innovation by the Numbers," Innovation.org, www.innovation.org/index.cfm/Toolsand Resources/FactSheets/Innovation_by_the_Numbers#6-PhRMA (accessed June 29, 2010).
7. Bloomberg Finance L.P.
8. See note 1.
9. Ibid.
10. Ibid.
11. Ibid.
12. Ibid.
13. Ibid.

14. Ibid.
15. Ibid.
16. Ibid.
17. Ibid.
18. Ibid.
19. Ibid.
20. Ibid.
21. Ibid.
23. Ibid.
24. Ibid.

Chapter 6: Challenges in the Health Care Sector

1. "IMS Forecasts Global Pharmaceutical Market Growth of 4–6% in 2010; Predicts 4–7% Expansion Through 2013," press release, IMS Health Incorporated, www.imshealth.com/portal/site/imshealth/menuitem.a46c6d4df3db4b3d88f611019418c22a/?vgnextoid=500e8 fabedf24210VgnVCM100000ed152ca2RCRD&vgnextfmt=default (accessed May 18, 2010).
2. Bloomberg Finance L.P.
3. Bristol-Myers Squibb 2006 Annual 10-K.
4. "Health Ministry Officially Publishes New NHI Medicine Prices in Japan," The Pharma Letter (March 17, 2008), www.thepharmaletter.com/file/18096/health-ministry-officially-publishes-new-nhi-medicine-prices-in-japan.html (accessed May 18, 2010).
5. See note 2.
6. "Settlement Agreement Between Merck & Co. Inc. and The Counsel Listed on the Signature Pages Hereto," (November 9, 2007), www.merck.com/newsroom/vioxx/pdf/Settlement_Agreement.pdf?bcsi_scan_34E336E4D93AA9DD=0&bcsi_scan_filename =Settlement_Agreement.pdf (accessed May 18, 2010).
7. See note 2.
8. Sharyl Attkisson, "Health Care Lobbyists' Rise to Power," CBS News (October 20, 2009), www.cbsnews.com/stories/2009/10/20/cbsnews_investigates/main5403220.shtml (accessed May 18, 2010).
9. Pfizer 2008 Annual 10-K.
10. Ibid.
11. Ibid.

Chapter 7: The Top-Down Method

1. Matthew Kalman, "Einstein Letters Reveal a Turmoil Beyond Science," Boston Globe (July 11, 2006), www.boston.com/news/world/middleeast/articles/2006/07/11/einstein_letters_reveal_a_turmoil_beyond_science/ (accessed December 10, 2009).
2. Michael Michalko, "Combinatory Play," Creative Thinking, www.creativethinking.net/DT10_CombinatoryPlay.htm?Entry=Good (accessed December 10, 2009).
3. Gary P. Brinson, Brian D. Singer, and Gilbert L. Beebower, "Determinants of Portfolio Performance II: An Update," The Financial Analysts Journal 47 (1991), 3.

4. Source: MSCI. The MSCI information may only be used for your internal use, may not be reproduced or disseminated in any form and may not be used to create any financial instruments or products or any indices. The MSCI information is provided on an "as is" basis, and the user of this information assumes the entire risk of any use made of this information. MSCI, each of its affiliates, and each other person involved in or related to compiling, computing, or creating any MSCI information (collectively, the "MSCI Parties") expressly disclaims all warranties (including, without limitation, any warranties of originality, accuracy, completeness, timeliness, noninfringement, merchantability, and fitness for a particular purpose) with respect to this information. Without limiting any of the foregoing, in no event shall any MSCI Party have any liability for any direct, indirect, special, incidental, punitive, consequential (including, without limitation, lost profits) or any other damages.
5. Ibid.
6. Ibid.
7. Ibid.
8. Ibid.

Chapter 9: Make Your Portfolio "Healthy"

1. Source: MSCI. The MSCI information may only be used for your internal use, may not be reproduced or disseminated in any form and may not be used to create any financial instruments or products or any indices. The MSCI information is provided on an "as is" basis, and the user of this information assumes the entire risk of any use made of this information. MSCI, each of its affiliates and each other person involved in or related to compiling, computing or creating any MSCI information (collectively, the "MSCI Parties") expressly disclaims all warranties (including, without limitation, any warranties of originality, accuracy, completeness, timeliness, noninfringement, merchantability, and fitness for a particular purpose) with respect to this information. Without limiting any of the foregoing, in no event shall any MSCI Party have any liability for any direct, indirect, special, incidental, punitive, consequential (including, without limitation, lost profits) or any other damages.
2. Thomson Reuters.

About the Authors

Michael Kelly is a Health Care Research Analyst at Fisher Investments. Michael graduated from Illinois State University with Bachelor of Science degrees in Finance and Marketing. He also has a Master of Science degree in Finance from Saint Xavier University. Michael holds CFA® and CFP® certifications. Originally from Quincy, Illinois, he currently resides with his wife Megan in San Mateo, California.

Andrew S. Teufel (San Francisco, California) has been with Fisher Investments since 1995, where he currently serves as a Co-President and Director of Research. Prior to joining Fisher, he worked at Bear Stearns as a Corporate Finance Analyst in its Global Technology Group. Andrew also instructs at many seminar and educational workshops throughout the US and UK and has lectured at the Haas School of Business at UC Berkeley. He is also the Editor-in-Chief of MarketMinder.com. Andrew is a graduate of UC Berkeley, and currently lives in San Francisco, California.

Index

Printed and bound by CPI Group (UK) Ltd, Croydon, CR0 4YY

27/10/2024

14580313-0001